LIVING ROOT

SUNY *series in*

Modern Jewish Literature and Culture

Sarah Blacher Cohen, editor

LIVING ROOT

A Memoir

MICHAEL HELLER

STATE UNIVERSITY OF NEW YORK PRESS

Published by
STATE UNIVERSITY OF NEW YORK PRESS, ALBANY

© 2000 State University of New York
All rights reserved
Printed in the United States of America

For information, address
State University of New York Press,
90 State Street, Suite 700, Albany, NY 12207

Production and book design, Laurie Searl
Marketing, Fran Keneston

Library of Congress Cataloging-in-Publication Data

Heller, Michael, 1937–
    Living root : a memoir / by Michael Heller.
        p. cm. — (SUNY series in modern Jewish literature and culture)
    Includes bibliographical references.
    ISBN 0-7914-4633-6 (alk. paper) — ISBN 0-7914-4634-4 (pbk. : alk. paper)
    1. Heller, Michael, 1937– 2. Heller, Michael, 1937—Childhood and youth. 3. Poets, American—20th century—Biography. 4. Jews—United States—Biography. I. Title. II. Series

PS3558.E4762 Z47 2000
811'.54—dc21
[B]
                                                                                          99-089096

10   9   8   7   6   5   4   3   2   1

For Tena,

who was there at the end of this story,

and for Bummy and Nick

Acknowledgments

I owe a debt of gratitude to a number of people who provided suggestions, counsel and feedback during the writing of this work, Jane Augustine, Larry Fixel, Anthony Rudolf and the late Armand Schwerner. My thanks to Tod Thilleman of Spuyten Duyvil Press for his help on the illustrations for this book. My thanks also to the SUNY Press production staff for their help and guidance in transforming the work into a book.

Portions of this work, some of it in different form, have appeared in the following magazines:

"From Living Root" by Michael Heller, published in *American Poetry Review*, Summer 2000.

"The American Jewish Clock" by Michael Heller, published in *Confrontation*, No. 50, Fall 1992.

"Living Root" by Michael Heller, published in *The Five Finger Review*, No. 15, 1996.

"Living Root" by Michael Heller, published in *The Jewish Quarterly*, Spring 1999.

"Living Root" by Michael Heller, published in *Parnassus: Poetry in Review*, Vol. 16, No. 2, 1991.

"Living Root" by Michael Heller, published in *Talisman*, No. 11, Fall 1993.

"Living Root" by Michael Heller, published in *TO: A Journal of Poetry, Prose and the Visual Arts*, Vol. 2, Nos. 3 and 4, Spring 1994.

A number of the poems in this work have been previously published as follows: "Bialystok Stanzas" first appeared in *Knowledge* by Michael Heller (SUN 1980). "In A Dark Time, On His Grandfather," "Constellations of Waking, "Some Anthropology," "The American Jewish Clock,"

"Mamaloshon" and "Accidental Meeting With An Israeli Poet" were published in *In The Builded Place* by Michael Heller (Coffee House Press, 1989).

I am grateful to the editors and publishers of the above publications for first presenting the work and for their kind permission to reprint it.

I would also like to thank the New York Foundation for the Arts for a Fellowship to complete the writing of this work.

Thus the Jew bends over his book, knowing in advance that the book always remains to be discovered in its words and in its silences.

—Edmond Jabès

A chronicler who recites events without distinguishing between major and minor ones acts in accordance with the following truth: nothing that has ever happened should be regarded as lost for history. . . . Each moment [mankind] has lived becomes a *citation à l'ordre du jour*— and that day is Judgment Day.

—Walter Benjamin

Semite: to find a way for myself

—George Oppen

I

*T*HE RITUALS: possibly the whole of one's Jewishness, except for God, could be squeezed, as from a vast sponge made of all time and space, into a few concentrated drops of liquid as ritual. Would these drops be honey or acid? For the memorialist in one's nature, they are, naturally, honey or amber, resinous substances that encase and preserve events until they have the dull finish of a minor detail in a painting by an Old Master. Yet for one like myself, who never fully came into belief, who has always felt in matters of religion both exposed and transgressive, the rituals are acid, each drop, as from a cosmic sponge, etching away the small certainties of personal history, corroding portions of the unsheltered self, that self which does not acknowledge God but which God might see, to burn like an open wound in air.

Such equivocal and painful feelings must have come early to me, probably as a result of an awareness of my mother's skepticism concerning matters of religion. For often, the ritual forms and objects of my child-hood, familiar as they were, comprised so many hand- and footholds for traversing the self's etched-out landscape, a *terra incognita* of hope and fear, of risk and parental admonition. As a child in the early nineteen for-ties, six or seven years old in Miami Beach, even as I sat, sunk deep in the velvet plush seats of Temple Emanuel on Washington Avenue, feeling the rapture of the ritual occasions, I sensed I was climbing a cliff face, the very physiognomy of otherness, the pathways of memory by which I skirted the fragile edging of the present. For me, then, the calendar of the Holy Days has always been a matter of nostalgia mixed with a deep, electric panic.

The rituals must occur in time and space—the duration of the Passover supper, for instance, with its stately movement of symbolic substances and courses, the bitter herbs, the matzos, the placing, with one's finger, of the red dots of wine onto the gleaming porcelain of the dinner plate. The child was thrilled: wine, plagues, blood, a transubstantial progression. In the America of the Forties, in my childhood, surrounded by the terrible hearsay of the Holocaust, the tale of Moses' deliverance, the marching out of Egypt (I saw it in my mind much as a Cecil B. DeMille would frame it: a winding, dusty band of Jews in loose flowing robes stretching from horizon to horizon), was a heroics, a portion of collective memory infused with hope.

As I recall, at this same time, as the century touched a near-bottomless void of evil and unspeakable cruelty, I was obsessed with the story of Gideon depicted in one of those Classic Comics of the Bible. The frames of the comic strip presented the story as a series of stirring visual drumbeats: Gideon builds, with his father's goods, with his father's bullocks and stands of trees, the altar to God, stealthily, at night. Gideon throws down his father's altar to Ba'al. And it is Gideon who, with the righteousness of youth, rebukes the Lord's angel: "O my Lord, if the Lord be with us, why then is all this befallen us?" Gideon's faith wavers; he demands of the Lord a sign. And again, an angel comes and with a touch of his staff, sets fire to the offering that Gideon has made. Now Gideon hears the voice of the Lord telling him that he, Gideon, shall be the instrument by which the Israelites will be set free. In the clear unambiguous cartoons of the comic book, in the edited speech forms of the dialogue balloons, there was a paradigm of revolutionary fantasy, one which all young people might entertain: to receive a divine call and to take from the corrupted elders and build a new, righteous, less oppressive world. The biblical cadence of Gideon's words as rendered in the King James Bible, which the comic book reproduced, his upbraiding of authority with its repeats of "Lord" and "us," astonished and disturbed me. It hinted at anguish but also justification. It even suggested some new pattern of relationship to my parents, who were, of course, Authority, thus implying to me the possibility of reason or of going beyond the blind willful reactions of childhood.

This story played in my mind against what I could intuit from my overhearings concerning the events in Europe. It entered into me physically, as though recoding the networks of my nerves. I was fascinated by the simple drawings in the comic book of the swords of Gideon and his band. The hilts of these swords, in the comic book artist's renderings, resembled those of well-made, functional butcher knives. Their simplicity was a strange lure to me, and over and over, sometimes consciously, though often unconsciously, I would doodle pencil drawings of the hilts in my notebook or on school paper. There were little ripples for finger grips on one side of these hilts, and as I drew, I could feel my hands closing around them. The sensation was so strong and vivid that I felt an immense empowering every time I was conscious of making such a drawing. The closest I had ever come to such a similar rush of energy occurred when I ran in the school playground, leaping up, half believing I would take off and fly like Superman.

While I was often curious about events in the Bible and asked questions of my Sunday School teachers, I felt absolute clarity on the story of Gideon and played his war games by myself in the nearby yards and parks. Under no circumstances was I going to discuss Gideon with adults, not with stern Rabbi Lehrman or ever-smiling Cantor Berkowitz whose Russian face was all knobby pink-blushed apples—those benevolent dictators of the Temple who, in their roles as our spiritual attendants, bred both affection and ambivalence. For the Law and the Book were in endless strife with the greensward of Flamingo Park and the horseplay of comrades. Gideon was my tale against the officious nature of spiritual duties; it was a tale against the Tale, which I could harbor as my secret and my plan. So it was that an older time could tell against the present if invoked as ritualized story.

Yet even as a child I associated narration with closure, with the last words of the small book a parent held, with its bright pictures and indulgent rhymes, the end of speaking and speaker, synonymous with the end of the child's day which was like death to me, when my mother left off reading me stories as I fell asleep. Here was such confused maelstrom of emotion: to come with heart beating to the story's end and yet to know it as *the* end. When I was very young, this hearing of my mother's voice seemed to produce a little orgasm, a flurry of deep hopes and sadnesses, which this stroking of the tympanum with sound and word had led to. The whole world crammed with a child's fantasies and distortions had been led in through the gate of the ear, that most feminine of organs. And even when I strained against fatigue, it seemed that my hearing was trying to reach out and clasp around this maker of sounds, this speaker who was my mother.

ZALMAN HELLER, my grandfather, Brooklyn, 1944. A rabbi in both Bialystok and New York City, he was given to declaiming the Jewish rituals in, to use Osip Mandelstam's phrase, "railroad prose."

The ritual story, the utterance from the Book of Books, transmitted from before the past had even begun, *in illo tempore*, as the anthropologists put it, was another matter. Such a story, timeless and eternal, had to be divine. Mantled in the sacred, it was meant to be heard and reheard, and, above all, to be pondered. Revelation was, by definition, didactic. As with *my* Gideon, it was meant to be rehearsed in private, in the crypts and fissures of personality where it had uses undreamt of by others. I was a well-behaved child as children go, at least that is how my parents so observed me; but secreted away in me where no one could look was all the black fury of generational difference, a blind will to grow which came together with parent, history, the wars and nights of terror in Europe. Story was its catalyst.

I return to the ritual supper, a sensorium of people and objects made blurry by sweetish wine. I remember now before me as in a dream the ceremonial lace of the table cloth, the crude, childish illustrations of the *Haggadah*, heavy brass of candlesticks, the brown and white stipples of the matzo. Tastes and sights. And yet these, strong as they are in memory, are not as powerful as the sounds I heard. More than anything else, I remember intonings: my grandfather's dronelike mumbling through prayers and instructions; later, my father's more clearly enunciated sounds.

For my grandfather, a rabbi and teacher, the whole ceremony, all ceremonies, were woven into one continuous chant, a swift, impelled, if muffled, music. A kind of absolute ease that alternately filled me with awe and fright. Safely sheltered by faith, his words could be uttered without impediment, without resistance to their very physicality, the puffs of accented breath, the glottals and dentals of their makeup. Even more, their semantic auras held no sway, it seemed, in my grandfather's consciousness as he recited them. This was very clear in the way he droned the passages, omitting all emphasis of meaning. To use the Russian poet Osip Mandelstam's phrase, my grandfather declaimed in "railroad prose," in the art of the sentence coupler. I had the impression that my grandfather felt his responsibility to these passages was *pro forma*, an unquestioning recital of God's command and that portion of God's mind which applied to the ritual supper.

My father's beliefs were less hard and fixed than his father's; he took more seriously each word, tried to feel its exactness, like a solid object held in his mouth, going in fear of the god he was far less comfortable with than was my grandfather. I, who am godless, took much from my father, including this legacy: to seek for the precise word, the secular word, which would deliver.

As a young boy, I had the childhood ambition to be good, to be godly, which meant I identified godliness with the speaking of the male line, the father and grandfather. But I also had a slight speech defect, a kind of *logos interruptus*, which shamed me, not only before the God I imagined then, but also before my mother, a teacher of speech, and so made me unworthy in my own eyes. In my tenth year, my mother, with perfect tact and gentleness, made light of this minor complication in my speech habits, sending me in a casual fashion to see the school speech teacher who effected some correction in my pronunciation. Yet like all children I lived with invented omens and invented codes, fears that transmuted to divine or parental law, and which in my mind separated me out from the rest. To this day I mangle certain words, transpose consonantals, suffer a kind of oral dyslexia, all of which mark me as of the tribe of the fallen. For years I felt reduced to silence whenever I came to a passage marked "In Unison" in the synagogue prayerbooks.

Stories and poems, not as entities, little narrative eggs, but as layers of sound on paper. In time, the reader goes from one closed loop of narration to another, hearing consonances and dissonances, resolving these or living in their irresolution. There are painful works yet to be written, not about how voices air their tales, but about how the books sit, adjacent to each other, about their cancellations and silences in the mind of a solitary reader.

Always, as I ruminated on my family and its past, I was listening to sounds, to rituals and voices, but I was hearing as well the faint music of closures, of one page laid over another, of a story that had to die so that later another might be voiced. What deadly quiet.

Walter Benjamin, that near-tragic wanderer in the German-Jewish diaspora who in a sense is the patron saint of this writing, wanted to "rub history against the grain." My own task here is rather similar, to rub story against story, to rub a life against the story's flow, to force time to jump the track of its well-grooved channel. Out of the dissonances in the stories comes the ambiguous conflict of allegiances, the deadened roots of decidedly imperfect Jewish and personal history, that text-game of time and religion, which beckons again and so wars with a cleansing present, that sleep of old reasons and memories obscured in the letterless sensate of now. How to reawaken?

In my mid-twenties, and with a sudden consciousness of beginnings, as though a new strange plant had begun to grow in my chest, in the throes of a psychic homelessness, that perpetual psychology of youth *cum* exile, I had attempted, when I first decided to be a writer, to build a house from the ashes of others, to find personhood, not in religion (my mother's atheistic leanings had forever sheared me off from belief) but in some lost ethnicity, ethnicity being to writers what patriotism is to the scoundrel.

In this endeavor, I am remembering that I was aided by my father, a fact which now strikes so curiously, since of all the members of the Heller family, it was he who in his youth had made the sharpest break with home, with religion and with his rabbi-father's heavy-handed authority. My father had invoked his own private diaspora, running away to sea at the age of fifteen, a Jewish Ishmael leaving my grandfather, a stern Ahab of a parent, on the shores of New York City.

I'm recalling now that it was in the early nineteen sixties on one of my periodic visits to Florida where my parents had moved that I first mentioned my literary intentions to my by then ailing father, run down and debilitated by the early stages of Parkinson's disease. True, I had been living and working in New York for some time, and I was twenty-six years old. But I still felt, almost as a tic or habit, a son's deference toward his father. My father had been no patriarch in the usual sense of that word. He had neither dominated at the dinner table nor sought to impose his will. His few temper tantrums, while memorable, mostly betrayed the frustration and desperation he'd bottled up over my mother's bad heart and his own downsliding fortunes. In my youth, when the family was moving piecemeal to Florida because of my mother's illness, there had been long periods of time when he was not present, having to remain in New York settling his business affairs.

So this faint desire to genuflect toward my father's presence had about it the quality of worshipping at an abandoned shrine, of *dovening* as if by rote over a dead book or false idol. That inherent falsity meant only that in wanting his blessing or judgment (either would have been extremely important to me then), I had agreed to conspire in mutual bad faith with the fictional roles of child and parent we had rarely inhabited. More than conspire, for the deep unending loneliness I felt as a child welled up whenever those roles threatened to dissolve, and I glimpsed through veils and curtains the blank emptiness of adulthood with its formless and open—and terrifying—spaces.

On the particular day in the mid-nineteen sixties that I am thinking about, bright and rounded with the Floridian spring sun, I had come armed from the North with a personal resolve bolstered by my winning a small but distinguished prize in poetry, and by the certain knowledge that I was quitting my job to go live in Europe for a year. It was just after mid-day, and my father was, as usual, half-asleep in the gloomy living room of our old apartment on Euclid Avenue in the south part of Miami Beach. The shades were pulled against the light, a comfort for him against the brightness, against the pain, it seemed to me, of living in a world circumscribed by his illness. I found him sunk in his beaten yellow easy chair, a tattered and frayed object which had become his personal redoubt. He was wearing one of his rumpled dark suits and a tie, and under the jacket an old stained cardigan buckled like a washboard at the buttons.

Such a scene, that chair especially, are emblematized in my memory. On another one of my visits, I was to paint him seated there, his hands resting on his thighs, his cocked head aslant the curved back that encircled him. A pencil moustache and a trim Van Dyke beard gave him an air of inscrutability. This watercolor hangs now in my study, my father's sleep-lidded eyes gazing down from the grainy paper over my desk where I write. Later, in the mid-seventies, in a moment of parental pride gone vaguely surreal, my mother traced out the design pattern that I had created for the cover of my first book of poems. From the design, she then cut pieces of avocado green terrycloth into a slipcover for my father's easy chair. Like a pop art or avant-garde monstrosity, my book jacket design was destined to balloon and bulge under my father's recumbent form. In the last months of his life, my father napped blissfully unawares like the statue of a crusader on a moss-covered tomb.

But to go back. On the day that I am thinking of, in the late spring of 1964, the time when I first presented myself as a writer to my father, he had, in his life, already embraced a placid illness-borne inertia, a complete and benign frame of reference that overlay or nudged to the periphery any waves of discomfort or irritation.

WATERCOLOR PORTRAIT by me of my father in his Miami Beach living room, 1978. "A pencil moustache and a trim Van Dyke beard gave him an air of inscrutability."

Speaking to him, I knew I would be awakening him from his semi-conscious stupor, from a mild but total numbness that had become his daily state. There would, of course, be no confrontation with him, of this I was sure, and I regretted deeply that I was not to experience one of those primal scenes which are an essential part of the substance and lore of the child's rebellion against the parent. Instead, I expected my father to take my words as he did so many other things at that time, with an almost ignoring tenderness, a mild haziness or befuddlement that seemed to wrap itself like a garment around every incident. I had watched him often as he beamed with a childish happiness at anyone who stood before him. I had watched as he gave up on "reading" people, on discerning their mood or intentions. Little by little, the tone of his personality was becoming more passive and withdrawn.

And yet still, perhaps in moments unawares even to himself, my father's facial features rippled with anger and loss. Such expressions were faint relics, mere hieroglyphs of rebellion, the body speaking beyond consciousness in a sign language that registered a protest against its own fate. Nostalgia, for instance, truly roused him. Recited memories or old songs from the past quickly brought tears to his eyes. Fear as well, when it broke through the shield of his placidity, suddenly electrified his being. It was in his eyes when he stared off into the depths of the room as into a future where only further waste and death loomed. And when his muscles no longer worked properly, when, for instance, he had to cross a busy street, terror suffused him and charged his motions. Suddenly, he no longer halted in his walk but resembled an antic ballet dancer, all tiptoes and odd high steppings, his legs moving in wild disjunctive arcs that made his progress even slower than his usual impeded gait.

So as I talked with him on that day, I was looking for signs, for something that would mark or commemorate the moment. And when I told him what I was going to do, to be a writer, to go away to Spain, I did detect a momentary flick of fright, but also a strange rolling back of his eyes, almost languid, as though under those drooping lids he could access other presences, other weighted phantoms necessary to his life. Then he nodded but said nothing. That moment, though I couldn't then formulate it, was bleak— harsh and generational in the sense that it was as marked and violent as the severing of the umbilical cord. There was a bit of hatred in it, the impersonal kind the dying can have for those who it appears will go on living. As well, I wasn't sure whether I had dashed unawares some specific plans my father had had for me which now left him bereft. Or had there been a kind of true transmission, one deeply tinged with his mortality and *his* unrealized hopes.

For my father, too, had had a writing "career," as he once abashedly denominated it to me. In his youth, in the many poems he composed and in little essays he wrote for the newspapers that he worked for, he had pitched his own language toward a sort of American romance, something he meant to be a poetic adornment upon the life of the young adventurer he had become at that time: runaway, soldier, railroad detective, movie director, lover. It was in his nature to favor clichés; they rang true, the way they so often do with young men of action. His faith in florid and pre-formulated bits of language, compounded in a grammar of effusive sentimentality, testified to his belief in the simplified essence of his words. They obviously had come easy to him, so that to say or write was to represent himself unambiguously, the hero of his own dime-store novel. And like his clumsiness with household repairs and machinery, they marked him as a nineteenth-century idler and dreamer, which in great part he was.

Later, toward the end of his life, this adornment in words, this emotional linguistic spillage was to flatten into a broad and stagnant delta of verbiage, muddied by the vocabularies and syntactical strategies of my father's public relations business and other assorted prosaic hucksterisms.

Looked at in its entirety, the descending path of my father's writing "career" reached its pitiable apotheosis, I suppose, in the last days of his working life. In the mid-nineteen seventies, while I was trying to become a writer, my father, despite his declining abilities, was, with my mother's encouragement, still trying to work. His senility, or was it Alzheimer's, had made it impossible for him to service or keep his clients.

It was then that my mother suddenly adopted my father's lifelong habits of fictionalizing. Fearing for his own loss of self-esteem or playing into the propensity for illusion making that had marked his adult life, she kept the offices of his public relations firm, Peter F. Heller Associates, open. She even retained, on a part-time basis, my father's aging secretary, Sara. Here, daily, my father napped in a big leather office chair for hours at a time, much as he did at home. Whenever he woke, Sara gave him a sheaf of freshly typed pages. These he would seem to scan, then nod approvingly. They contained lists from old address books, names of people who had died or moved away. While Sara and my mother looked on, my father haltingly enunciated each name on the list. Together, the two women had conspired to present these as fresh work to him and were now reaping a harvest of garbled sound.

My mother, almost always restrained, nearly wept as she told me of these sessions in the office. And when I visited the premises, everywhere I saw these piles of useless addresses, typed and retyped in long neat columns onto good bond paper. My father's language had reached its near-entropic end in this roll-call of the invisible, the out-of-town and the recently dead.

Still later, when he was in the nursing home and no longer recognized me as I entered the room, he'd often call me by someone else's name, possibly a name from those very lists. This was the beginning of the last phase of his having language, when, in the nursing home, he could no longer make phrases nor sometimes even words. The sounds that came from his mouth merely joined in some horrible synchronicity with all the other noise of the universe unmarked by human intelligence or will.

The pain of witnessing my father's utter helplessness filled me with anguish. That he no longer could communicate betokened an even more terrible kind of reversal: a fundamental reversion or degradation of spiritual material, of what constituted his being human, slowly transmuting itself into the inertness of matter. For language and utterance have a certain expectative quality, a strange momentum and impellance that both animates and lies along the plane of one's intentions and even destinies, something we know from our own readings and listenings. That endless entwining which bound us together and which had been spun out by my father's words and by our conversations, was now snapped.

My father wanted to be a writer. In the sixties, in the early stages of his illness—possibly in that very moment when I was telling him of my hopes and desires—I imagine that my father sensed not only his soon-to-be-blunted past but the possibility of his son's completing certain unfinished flights of language which he had already begun.

After I told my father of my writer's hopes, he tentatively urged me on, as though any success I might have as a writer were stirred into the soupy gall of his own disappointments. He advised me to secure a bilingual Yiddish-English history of Bialystok (the small city in Poland from which my family fled) that had been compiled and written by a friend of his, David Sohn, also a Bialystoker. Bialystok, my father continually reminded me with some pride, was where *we* had come from. In those last difficult years of his life, when memory waned and a tide of confusions broke over him, the name of his birthplace, as a definitive marker in his utterance, dragged like an anchor in sand. And that I might come to be a chronicler of Bialystok may also have made more bearable to him my desires to be a writer. There would be a strained pleasure if I were to be led by his suggestions and enthusiasms, much the way a teacher may take rueful pride in a student who, in following the dictates of his own education, surpasses the professor's original scholarly pursuits.

Sohn's book, *Bialystok: Photo Album of a Renowned City and Its Jews the World Over*, replete with many drawings and historical photographs as well as text, was indeed a gold mine of material. To my vague and unformed end of becoming a writer, I secured a copy of this book, this "official" chronicle of Bialystok, from the New York Bialystok Center on Manhattan's Lower East Side. This was in early 1963, and the crumbling pavements of Henry Street and East Broadway could be likened to an urbanized airport lounge. The old Jews were embarking, moving or dying out of the soot-blackened tenements that lined the streets, while the recently disembarked Hispanics and the Asian overflows of Chinatown were marching slowly up the blocks to take their places. It was an urban enclave of manifest tensions, one which exhibited a vocabulary of push and shove in every voice and gesture. I had driven to the Center in my new Volkswagen, and no sooner had I parked on East Broadway, than a group of youths wearing *yarmulkes*, black pants and white shirts, surrounded my car and started beating on the roof with their fists, shouting "Nazi Gas Wagon!" After a few minutes, while I huddled in my seat, banging back at them on the windows in a mood close to hysteria, they left off and wandered down the street. The thumping of those hands on metal? There was no more power there than in that of the little breeze a page makes when it is turned over. One turns pages back, one pores over history, but the writing remains fixed as on a tombstone. Wasn't that hatred, twenty, thirty years displaced, the ink of this century?

Bialystok. It was my naive intention to write a historical novel. And the book I acquired, fully illustrated and with its pages half in Yiddish and half in English, was to be my way in, a catwalk bridging cultural and semantic universes, a walkway over the spaces of time, from which, as I mentally sounded out the text and pictures, odd dissonances were heard as though a stiff and antique notepaper were being crumpled. In those barely muffled disputations of sound or image, my postadolescent desires to have an identity and yet to be released from the shackles of any tradition I did not elect for myself were somehow joined. The novel never did materialize, but Sohn's book gave me many satisfactions and ultimately led me to poetry. I think of it now, and for part of what I am writing here, using it again, only this time as a template to lay over a clean piece of paper so that in some sense I may compel memory and history to coincide.

In the book, as I look at it again, many of the older photographs, because of their poor quality, lend themselves all too well to my purposes. These show

BIALYSTOK before World War II. "Nostalgia . . . inevitably colored sepia."

mostly street scenes or portraits and group photos of the town's eminent figures. Yet the close-in details of a face or of a building appear to have been blotted up by time or, at the least, by the heavy hand of the retoucher. To contemplate them is to slowly slip from actuality to fable, to dwell in the swabbed dreamy spaces of remembrance as though history itself were beckoning one to lean one's head into a fuzzed fantasy of events. Nostalgia, especially in its cheapest, most sentimental form, is inevitably colored sepia.

And yet—and herein lies my need—because of the peculiar fate of those born into twentieth-century European Jewish culture, such material is poised on a knife-edge in time, the meeting place of old memories, of rituals and traditions, and of catastrophe. The photographs, the records and accounts, are, at once, the stuff of nostalgia or terror depending on how one lets them become entangled in the webs of time. In this sense, any act of memory is cautionary, less about reconstructing a past than about construing a future.

I am remembering then, not for the sake of *what was*, but in a sense, in order *to be*. In this, the Bialystok book was less of an aid to memory than, as philosophers might say, a *res potentia*, an empowering, even occult, object. Opening its rather glossy pages or merely contemplating the rather awful cream and brown letterings (they were both in English and Yiddish) of its cover, put me in a heightened, strangely receptive state of mind. And what about the facts, the dates, the names?—the reader may righteously ask. They too took on a new importance, not as facts but as planetary bodies or constellations, having about them fixed or immutable, but necessarily nonhuman, laws of motion. Freud wrote of dreaming that "there is at least one spot in every dream at which it is unfathomable—a navel, as it were, that is part of its contact with the unknown." In the memoir, that scripted dream-time of a past, other lives, parents and relatives, one's enemies and friends, the cities and places we have lived in and experienced, these are the "navels" of waking life, things that cannot be made different or revised. They function, not as determinants, however, but as anchorages or ports of call, occasions from which spread an immense totality of facts and potentialities beyond any knowing or imagining, which, rather than define, await me in the future. The law of their organization, like the billions of computer calculations needed to determine the location of an atom in a thunderstorm, must remain a mathematical mystery, and thus, any order I impose on this totality is a function, not so much of truth or "identity," but of artfulness. Nothing in the calculus of possibility is, strictly speaking, recollected or forgotten under the sign of cause or necessity. Even as we would want to see ourselves as voluntary figures, living finally beyond history or mastering it, what we discover as soon as we reflect is that our past is innovation.

I remember, as I have said, in order *to be*: My family had come from that thriving whirlpool of Middle European-Jewish activity centered in

Russian-Polish Bialystok. How long they had lived there or from whence they had come before that time, I have no idea. When the Jewish community in Bialystok was destroyed in World War II, not only did a way of life vanish but an entire written history flamed into smoke and ash.

From what I have been able to learn, my great-grandfather David, from whom I acquired my middle name, was an important rabbi of the city, much loved by the populace for opening his house to the poor and to lost strangers coming through town. He was revered and spoken of in the family in hushed tones. His son, my grandfather, Zalman Heller, a rabbi, teacher, and sometimes writer, fleeing the pogroms and poverty of Central Europe, arrived in New York in 1911. By 1913, the entire family, his wife Rose, his sons, among them my father Pete (then called Philip), his brother Nat, and the daughters, Mildred (who was always called Jen), Ina, and Bea, were all living in the Williamsburg section of Brooklyn. A photograph of Zalman Heller in the Bialystok volume (published in 1951) has this caption: *Zalman Heller: Hebrew-Yiddish writer and educator. Of the first members of the Hebrew-Language Society in Bialystok. He is now Principal in a Brooklyn, N.Y. Yeshivah.* Beyond these bare outlines of arrival and emplacement, what has come to me is mainly folklore and oral history.

The house where the family lived in Bialystok, my Aunt Jen told me, was somewhat primitive. Cheap pine furniture, crude plumbing, muslin drapes, my aunt enumerated its humble inventory. At mealtimes, she remembered, food was ladled into hollowed out recesses chiselled into the wooden top of the dining table, as dishware was mainly for the wealthy. After a meal, boiling water was poured over the greasy concavities to cleanse and prepare them for the next meal. Details like this were not so much information but part of the jargon of remembrance, a mode of talk that bent itself romantically aslant of factuality. And now, such recited information seems even more highly colored and shaped by external influences, the costumed historical movie epics I saw as a child, history book illustrations, comics, and the like until the form of my family's life in Europe resembles a medieval tale.

From my early desires to be a writer, my own mind has surely flooded these near-mythological designs with dreamings and nostalgias. To ground these fantasies I first conjured up those sepia realities of the illustrated Bialystok history book. I recall having searched its pages in vain for a picture of my great-grandfather, either depicted singly or in the various groupings of Rabbinical Associations, Fire Departments, and Concerned

Educators. In the book, he remains bodiless and faceless, inscribed only in the words that describe his deeds and in the furnished scenery of his environment, nineteenth-century Bialystok's few newly paved streets and public monuments.

As a young person, I had been free to invent him physically, and so, because he had been likened to a saint, my earliest imaginings were of a tall figure in nondescript clothes with a white-bearded face. As I had read geography books and seen movies in which the forests and cultivated fields of Eastern Europe were described, I dressed the figure in peasant garb, loose fitting shirts, wide leather cinch belts, trousers tucked in boots, a cap of some sort. Such imaginings had more than physiognomic consequences. I created a vague psychology and set of behaviors for my great-grandfather, not that I thought in those adult, educated terms but that the clothes suggested a way of life, an actual place of habitation, a whole concatenation of inferences by which I built up an invented past. Nor does such an invention endstop with a vision of the past. Saintliness, peasants, labor, a rural world, these had not only their pastness but their presentness for the boy who conjured them. Certain modes of being, desires, valuations were projected out of the imagined goodness and way of life of David Heller onto the impressionable mind of the great-grandchild, Michael (middle name David), already propelling him toward a future which even as it was unknown, held as one of its principles the invisible structure of desire which this invented past contained.

It was only when a few years ago my uncle Nat gave me a photograph of great-grandfather David, that certain illusions were both dispelled and, uncannily, confirmed. That is, this sole surviving photograph of David Heller and his wife Fanny only adds to the irresolvable nature of my past. In the picture, the couple are seated on a wicker bench in what appears to be a formal garden with marble vases and trellises behind them. Of course, the background with its camera-lens-induced flatness could simply be a painted screen, as was often the custom, in which case no conclusions could be drawn about the house in which they lived. They are well dressed, though David Heller is wearing something of the same costume with which my childhood fantasy clothed him: boots into which his trousers are tucked, a countenance framed by a dark well-trimmed beard on its way to becoming all white. The near-symmetry between the photograph and my fantasizing is curious and unaccountable, as though rather than a triumph over time, the photograph only confirmed the secretive powers we label

MY GREAT GRANDPARENTS, David and Fanny Heller,
Bialystok, before 1900. The ambiguities of this
photograph "only confirmed the secretive powers we label
prophecy and forebodings."

prophecy and foreboding; it is as though the genetic material of which I am composed held, if mildly mutated, the visual information which my grandfather Zalman and his son Peter, my father, must have pored over, possibly discussed together and been moved by.

Further, when examined closely, the photograph is somewhat at war with the idealizing vernacular of my own visual imagination. Fanny's hair stylishly pulled back, David's full beard neatly trimmed, these, along with the cleanliness of the clothes, imply urbanity and even sophistication, ways of being somewhat at odds with my childish preconceptions of the saintly. The hands of both are small as though given to delicate rather than manual labor. It is hard to associate the house described by my aunt, the cheap furniture and primitive kitchen, with those hands. Thus, the net effect of this photograph is to cast doubt on some of the information I have acquired about my grandfather from the minor historical musings of my family. If a picture is worth a thousand words, it is also quite capable of denying another thousand already spoken or imagined. The truly efficacious words or pictures are those that come as revelations or epiphanies and so overcome mere pictures and mere words.

Yes, epiphanies. The British writer, Neal Ascherson, in his account of modern-day Bialystok, reminding the reader of its near-total destruction in World War II, touches on the lugubrious sight of the old Jewish cemetery with no one alive left to tend it, a place where, he writes, "oblivion is infinitely deeper." Without Jewish mourners and rememberers, the cemetery in its ruination is an indescribably alien presence, a rock-strewn outcropping memorializing only indifference, horror, and moral failure. Here and there the old Polish antisemitism still flares up, its object virtually an absence. Bialystok, Ascherson tells us, was at the crossroads of any number of cultural-linguistic entities, Polish, Byelorussian, Jewish; among its more well-known inhabitants was Ludwik Zamenhof, the inventor of Esperanto. It was also the home of the Jewish hero Melmud who threw sulfuric acid at the face of an SS man during the final ghetto uprising. Absences and erasures.

Ascherson describes a Poland leached of its Jews by the Nazis, yet of Jews who still float, force-fields of epiphanies, through the nightmares of Polish villagers, of Jews who still dance on the glossy surfaces of old photographs.

⁂

For me, then, as I think about the history of my family, two inter-twining teleologies are at work: one a poetics of memory constructed around a class of near-physical objects, photographs, letters, scraps of talk, images. The other is the principle of montage as Walter Benjamin tried to bring it over into historical analysis, "to detect," he writes, "the crystal of the total event in the analysis of the simple individual moment." Montage sunders the purposeful chains of chronicle, those stories that mandate "official" sense and "official" views. Thus, everywhere I look at or remember a past, chronicle is broken open into contradictions and ambi-guities so that another logic is impelled, one that builds contrary to the flow of time. These shards or planes of broken time, each with its con-tributory weights and experiences, form the shaky house of cards of iden-tity. The shifted meanings, in their re-occurrences, no longer build into a story, for they are no longer under the power of time. Instead, like a con-stellation of words, a poem, for instance, they re-form as some metonymic name or word, some David or Michael. To which I would add one more consideration, that for our words to so name, one must have a faith in intelligibility as though something of our own planular ghosts were not mere hauntings but ways of flying on words into others, embracing and dissolving together, an Esperanto of the spirit. On what else do we base the word *hope*?

David Heller's life, in such a faceted obduracy, even as it was praised by my aunts and uncles, troubled and puzzled them. There were aspects of that life to which they could not connect. Though they often mentioned his rabbinical piety and his good deeds, these references were short and fleetingly passed over as though dwelling too long on his charity would poison their own genteel acquisitiveness. In effect, as if to confirm his holiness, David Heller's life was a mystagogic presence among my rela-tives. It baffled them with its strange hints and flashes of the atemporal power of compassion. Like any deeply moral story, it affected the mem-bers of the Heller clan, confronting their sense of the appropriate unfold-ing and rationality of time, their investment in logic, in respectability and, as they might have put it, their need for a "decent" standard of living.

Only my Aunt Jen, my father's oldest sister, who had been a "Wob-bly" and later died in a mental home, spoke at any length about David, and then, her own vulnerable mental state enabled the other relatives to discount her words, to *shush* her if she spoke too long in their presence.

That Aunt Jen should be the broken-voiced chronicler of the only Heller "saint" is especially apt. Much of what I heard about David Heller was communicated to me by her during the summer before I went to college when I lived in my Aunt Jen's and Uncle Charlie's house in Island Park, New York. I had found summer work at the nearby beach clubs in Long Beach, and Charlie and Jen let me rent, for a few dollars a week, the bare wooden cage of a room in their unfinished attic.

Jen, of all the sisters, was the most friendly toward my father though she shared the family view of him as a *tummler* whose waywardness had brought him in his later years little financial reward. Pete was younger, but he was endeared to her even for his foibles, which, at least, in her eyes, made him seem less "bourgeois" than the rest of the family.

Jen, like so many lower-middle-class Americans, had nearly been struck down by the Depression. Charlie, her husband, had been a truck driver in the years before the Crash but had been let go in 1930. He'd found a job operating a taxi, but there were few New Yorkers on the city streets who could afford to hail a cab. There was never any money.

Jen, the oldest child in the family, remembered the pogroms of Bialystok, and the tales of the Tsar's cossacks who swept out of the East to pillage the Jews of Belorussia. Had she fled all that to starve amidst the untold abundances of America? Like many, she was drawn toward left-wing politics, toward socialism and even communism. She had a beautiful singing voice, and joined the chorus of the IWWOW, the "Wobblies," and sang the *Marseillaise* and the *Internationale* at the great union halls on 14th Street and Irving Place in Manhattan. The world of the Thirties, the creation of capitalists and warmongers, ravaged at their door, but Jen was determined to make that world a better place.

At the Depression's heights, when she and Charlie were desperately broke, my father was, for one of the few times in his life, gainfully employed as a newspaperman on the *Brooklyn Eagle*. On Sundays, he visited his sister, turning up with a gift basket of groceries at her cramped apartment in Middle Village, Queens, where she lived with Charlie and their two young boys, Murray and Robbie.

In the early 1940s, I too was taken on these visits and remember playing with my cousins in the darkness of those little rooms, the trapped smells of cheap meals and the tattered overstuffed furniture of the living room which seemed to leave no space for people. The cemeteries of Middle Village were one of New York City's major burial grounds, and the windows of Jen's and Charlie's apartment looked out over acres of graves. Sitting on a couch in the living room, eating in the kitchen or gazing out from the bedroom windows, one saw stone after stone in irregular rows pitched upward toward the sky. Today, I think of that necropolis, that counter-city of the dead with its weedy parklike walks and trodden-down knolls, lying in particular desolation opposite my living relatives.

Years later, when I saw Jen and Charlie again in Island Park, it was clear that the day-to-day fears and grinding poverty of the Depression had exacted a terrible toll on Jen. During the Thirties, she had developed a severe case of insomnia, and was unable to sleep for fear of what she would have to face when she awakened. This habit had carried over into her later years, and in Island Park, in that brief summer before my college semester began, I was aware that she often stayed up at night sewing and mending while she watched television until five or six in the morning. Only in the growing light of the day would she drag herself to her room for a few hours of precarious sleep. Fearing that any excess sound would arouse her, she instructed me that when I awoke in the morning I was to run as little water as possible from the taps and to leave my urine and feces floating in the toilet for her to flush later when she woke up.

Jen, who had once been slim and good-looking, was now, in her late sixties, short and obese. When she spoke, one could see only one large tooth in the front of her mouth; it seemed to break up her speech into fractured presences, into shards of linguistic matter which spilled at random and lay across the planes of meaning like broken tablets. Often she communicated in grunts or guttural shouts, rebuking Charlie as a poor provider or for leaving his dirty coffee cups around the house. I was berated for minor household infractions, for being worthless and a capitalist (at the time, I planned to work after graduation as an engineer for a large corporation), for leaving a window ajar and letting the wet marshy air of Rockaway Bay steal into the house.

On my day off from the beach club, while Charlie was driving his cab in the city, I drove Jen into Long Beach to do her marketing. Such expeditions spiralled back into her nightmares where every exchange of money induced paranoia and outrage. At the supermarket checkout counter, while people behind us fumed and cursed, Jen went over and over the price of each item with the embarrassed clerk, making sure it had been properly entered on the register slip. In the butcher's, Jen picked up and slapped down slices of meat on the countertop. Hurling insults, she insisted that each purchase be weighed twice on the different scales in the store. Shaking her fist in his face, she made the butcher take her back into the refrigerated meat lockers so that she could see the blue inked stamps with their Hebrew letters on the hanging slabs of meat which showed that they were indeed properly kosher. Once home, all the supermarket goods were put on the kitchen table and again checked off one by one against the register slip while Jen wailed imprecations at the great antisemitic A & P stores, those war profiteers who sold tainted meat to the army troops and had once made sick her older boy Murray in the Signal Corps.

An intensity of fear mingling with ancient furies permeated the house; it wafted in now and then, like the rank smell of the oil slicks on the bay. My aunt, her mind crowded with the ravening birds of recent history, had trouble distinguishing between the real and the imaginary. The TV in the living room, which was never turned off, became the central antagonist in her life. If one of the soap operas was on, Jen, walking across the room, shouted warnings to one character about the villainy of another. At night, on the evening news, Eisenhower became Satan, excoriated for America's imperialism and expansionist tendencies. And Khrushchev, whose unkempt roundnesses Jen had begun to resemble, was beseeched to bring the heavens down on America or to cure the ills of a thousand dictators around the world, from Rockefeller to Franco.

When the living room became unbearable, Charlie headed for the basement, to tinker or develop pictures with his photographic equipment. I grabbed a book off the shelves, usually a fat red volume from the World's Great Books, one of my aunt's prized possessions, and stole away to the attic. That attic room trapped and held the day's heat; from its unfinished risers of new pine, the sharp, astringent odor of resin baked off into the sticky air. I lay, sweating on my bed, with Montaigne or Plato in my hands, my thumbs leaving dark welts of moisture across the page. It seemed I was trying to follow a thought while below the turmoils of the world raged in my aunt.

On those wilting summer nights, as I lay trapped in the stifling heat of my room, the graceful formulations of words, the smooth, keen prose of the classicists, seductive as they were, began to slip away from me. Those elegant, symmetrical formulations were insufficient to the world I lived in and my head hurt from the battle between what was written whole and what I heard that was fragmentary and broken.

Now, as I read in my classical dictionaries about the Sibyl of the ancient world who uttered prophecies, I think of Aunt Jen. Scholars have assumed that until the fourth century B.C., there was only one Sibyl, but that then, in the centuries that followed, many began to appear, speaking in different tongues and perhaps with the riddled speech of mad diviners and savants. Aunt Jen was of that latter tribe. Her keening was a belated harangue to History and to the endless acres of gravestones she had lived beside.

Surely, contemporary literature, first as I read it and then came to write my own, has given itself over to this sibylline element, speaking its truths and foretellings in dislocations and disjunctions. As I think back, remembering the summer I spent with Aunt Jen while finishing college, I am reminded that it was in the interstices of her uttered fragments that Bialystok and the Hellers I write about came into being.

BIALYSTOK STANZAS
(from a book of old pictures)

1

Light—
The scene filled with photographer's light

This sparsely furnished room
In the corner of which
A china-closet Ark

The old men
Under green shaded bulbs
Reading *Torah*
The prayers are simple,
To what they think larger

Than themselves
—the place almost bare,
Utterly plain

The flat white light
Adds no increment
But attention

2

He sits in the armchair
Beside his bed

In his hands
A Yiddish paper

On his head
A high black
Pointed *yarmulke*

The room's things
Furnished by donation
Reads a small brass plaque
Above the headboard of the bed

A bed, a hat upon his head

A *yiskor* glass, the candle for the dead
Burnt down, the wax scraped out
He uses it for drinking

3

Shiny linoleum
You can almost
Smell the pine oil

The beds
A few feet apart

So the old men
Tired of the world
In the evening
Can face each other
And talk

But now the shades are half pulled up
Sun streams in the windows
The room almost empty
But for the two directors
Sitting stiffly on chairs
Who, like the white painted beds,
Seem supremely official

At one side
Two grey bedridden men
Finished too with dignity
Are giggling

                    4

The old bind with phylacteries
—between the leather turns
The pinched flesh bulges, the old
Skin, the hairs burn

As if to do this is also
For the pain
—to explain
To Him of what it is
They are made

Thus, why they fail

5

This one and that one
Look like madmen
With their long wisps of hair

They scream: I chant, I dance
Like a crab

In the room the women wail
A plangent erotic note
Their loins itch with double fire
As he in topcoat-who-is-blessed
Bestirs them
Screams their demons back

Until their innocence
Stands naked as desire

Oy, Oy
He whirls, he spins
Till the beard is out
From his face like a flag

And in wild wisdom
Throws her to the boards
She, who would
That next instant
Have pulled him down to her
But for the trick
Of the ritual

6

THE JEWISH FIRE COMPANY

There was one fireman none knew
Neither his family nor friends

He had good eyes, though they looked
A little wild. He was sent
To the watchtower

One day, almost at once,
Two fires broke out in town
The hasid grocer's
And a gentile butcher

The fireman warned
Of the butcher's blaze
But said nothing about the grocer
Whose place burned to the ground

When what he had failed to do
Was discovered and explanation demanded
He said: those who do not
Follow our God's way
Must be helped
And those who do
Must accept his justice

This one joined
So the young ladies
Should see him in uniform

They did
And flattered the brass and leather
But not him

Finally, he charmed a farm girl
Of pious family into the fields

And in the manner of the orthodox
Threw his cap to the hay
Where he thought to take her

To his delight, she bent toward
The straw, raising her skirt
As she kneeled. Suddenly,
She whisked the cap up
Tucked it in her girdle and ran away

So ashamed was he
The next day he left town for Warsaw

Years later, the farm girl
Placed the cap on her first-born's head

7

TERRIBLE PICTURES

Page 147

Snow—
A group of people
Awkwardly caught

They have just discovered
The photographer, and he, them

The old man with the sack
Who has turned
Shrugs his disbelief into the lens

No sense of emergency
In the pose
Could be as real

Page 153

Grimly
They lie closely packed
Upon each other
In the mass grave

Looking now
Like figures of saints
Carved across cathedral doors

—but beyond image or irony,
The empty wrongness.

Here, all death
Was made untimely

Page 163, Caption:

"fought in the streets to the very end
and perished by his own hand
with the last remaining bullet"

Page 164, Caption:

"died in the ghetto"

Page 166, Caption:

"fell in battle . . . 1944"

Page 168, Caption:

"killed . . ."

Page 157, Burnt Synagogue

This light—
A river through which
Another life poured

Figure and ground
Of how the dark
Informs the light

Brings forth bodies, faces
Brings forth
The things of the earth
That we see to completion
—beloved, hated—

But that life was broken forever
Here, look, look, this is but
Its mirror

Only the mirror remains

And gone—
Whole peoples are gone
To horror beyond remonstrance—

Freitogdige
Donershtogidige
*Shabbosdige**
Consumed in those fires

Words can add nothing
That flame itself was without a light

8

FROM THE ZOHAR

The blue light
    having devoured
All beneath it:
    the priests,
The Levites, etc. . . .

------

*The Yiddish names above were those given by the citizens of Bialystok to the victims of three mass executions: "the Friday dead," "the Thursday dead," "the Saturday dead."

Now the prayerful ones
Gather
    at the flames' base
Singing and meditating
    while above the lamp glows,
The lights in unity are merged
Illumined world
    in which above and below
Are blessed

9 (Coda)

One God. One boiled egg.
Thirty *dy-yanus*, and the Paradise
Not yet given a number.

Eight nights, eight lights
Which break the dark
Like a cat's wink.

I think the boot is not gone—
Whose boot? I ask
Do you wear the boot?
Or does he who wears the boot
Wear you?

Coat of my pain, cloth
Of pain, winding sheet of
My horror. Just a rag,
Just a *shmata*. You
are not my pain, not you.
My pain is me: I am the Jew.

Even as I feel the dark specific weight of a lost Bialystok, I find myself
mulling over a passage from Olivier Revault D'Allonnes's gem of a book,
Musical Variations on Jewish Thought. "The characteristics," he writes, "by

which Jewish thought is infallibly recognized is that it grasps every object as non-obligatory and inconclusive in itself, as an object whose worth is set by its counterpoint, even in cases where its counterpoint is nothing." The endlessness of biblical commentary, which marks not some aspect of Jewish religious practice but is that practice virtually in its entirety, exhibits Revault D'Allonnes's recognition. The history of the Jews as given in the Pentateuch, half "fact" and half "fiction" or "legend," establishes primarily, via this very indeterminancy, the possibility of endlessly being rethought. Time, even narrative time, is a series of musical phrases, repeated motifs, rises that later fall, and falls that climb to new heights. I wanted to be a writer, a memorialist, I once jotted down in my notebook; I would look back, not even aware that such looking placed everything that ever happened in one context and one context only: infinitude. So then, what was anything: a rule, a life, a book?

When I began seriously to write poetry some seven or eight years after I had started and abandoned my "Bialystok" novel, I had turned again to the Bialystok book; hence the parenthesis "(from a book of old pictures)" under the poem's title. The sequence as a whole of "Bialystok Stanzas" seems now to have been governed by a number of coincidental interests, Walter Benjamin's notion of the photograph as the "posthumous moment," the Kabbalistic ideal of Devekuth or "adhesion" which is itself surrounded by notions of light and seeing, and the need to articulate, specifically in the "TERRIBLE PICTURES" section, that which can not be put into words, the Holocaust. In this regard, "light" as that which makes things visible and intelligible, and as the play of imaginative possibility, was the central idea hovering over every element of the poem, including the black light of the "Burnt Synagogue," in the fires of which the poignant Jewish illumination of the religious life was consumed. Section 9, the coda of the poem, incorporates some words and phrases of my grandfather which were uttered at a seder he and my family attended in Florida shortly before his death. At the time, he was in his eighties, perhaps suffering from the senile dementia that afflicted him in his late years.

My first thoughts of poetry had been imaginings of tattered scraps of language sewn together, tending to sound like an uninflected music in the manner of my grandfather's lengthy, ritualistic monologues with God. I

knew music, and perhaps poetry, were made of notes, the child's prover-
bial "black birds" strung on telephone wires as depicted for me in second
grade music class. But my grandfather's way of reciting appeared to take
no notice of these birds; his voice hummed out the very wires themselves
along which minuscule pulses ran. God was at the end of those wires, at
those infinite horizons where the parallel lines met. And besides, God's
birds were not crows or ravens, a gentile friend told me, but sparrows.

Thinking back, I know I had no firm conception of poetry as a child,
or at least I only vaguely remember its impingement as one does Mother
Goose and Jabberwocky. There was, however, the indirect influence of my
cousin Arthur, seven years older, who lived with us and was acknowledged
the smartest person in the house. Arthur's parents had both died of can-
cer when he was still young, and he had made it part of his mission in life
to track down the killers of his parents. If childhood has its labyrinths and
cul-de-sacs, adolescence and young adulthood furnish these blunted passages with their character and texture. Arthur, in his teens, lived with a
formidable sense of purpose. He formed a powerful interest in chemistry;
he was a teenage knight preparing for battle with the malignant dragon
that had slain his parents and now lay in wait in the dark fastnesses of
some other human body, possibly his, while he studied. Arthur would go
on to take degrees in biochemistry at Harvard and Antioch, and to head
up a research laboratory.

During those years Arthur lived with us, he brought home glass-stop-
pered retorts and beakers, the pieces of fragile tubing and pipettes from
the school lab. They lay about on the shelves of the bookcases and on his
desk. If a door slammed or the wind buffeted the house, a faint tinkling
music could be heard through the rooms. And when the sun came through
the windows, the light danced along the shiny, brilliant edges of the glass-
ware and stainless steel as though glancing off armor.

It was in high school that Arthur became interested in politics, in particular the catalytics of revolution and struggle. Pamphlets of Marx and
Engels, Lincoln Steffens and Thomas Paine were scattered throughout
the house, in those McCarthy era days, constantly irritating my mother.
Now and then, Arthur invited some of his high school friends to discuss
politics over dinner. The rest of the family would be banished from the
dining room while Arthur and five or six of his friends consumed nine or
ten tasty fried chickens, mashed potatoes and biscuits made by Blanche,
our black maid, washing all of it down with quart after quart of chocolate

milk. The "discussion" over, the group would go lie down on the living room carpet, sighing and burping like seals in the zoo.

At other times, Arthur often stood over me and declaimed from political tracts, from left-wing magazines and newspapers, the terminologies and jargons striking my ears as gibberish. This, and the dining room talk I overheard, and of which I was no part, for I often simply stood outside the entrance to the room and listened, were, in my memory, the first words I heard about politics. While the subjects of this talk I remember only dimly, the "soundings" of it left a negative impression upon me. All my deep instinctive feelings about language up until that time were that words were communications *between* people, words of speakers which had some impact or consequence for me. I found my own hopes and fears situated in the speech of my parents or friends. When adults discussed my mother's bad heart, for instance, my whole body trembled like a seismograph as it registered the tonal vibration of every verbal nuance.

In hearing the uttered rituals of the Temple, or in reading the tales of the Bible and history and in young people's fiction, I seemed to undergo morphological changes as I fantasized and in a sense shared my consciousness with tales of heroism and evil. The psychic imprintings of verbal entities were most powerful, for they seemed to shunt past the present-day world and so reached a certain, though ill-formed, metaphysical depth in me. The words of authors—and the greatest author of all was God— formed themselves out of immeasurably distant sources as though one were perceiving a writing in the sky. And, as words from Heaven or as the brilliant black ink of books, they simply replaced one's mind with that of an imperious Other.

Arthur, by contrast, and through my overhearing, introduced me to a language that was about people, indeed, *for* people, not me or my close ones, but people in general, people everywhere as though they existed before us in a landscape or were part of some enormous machine. These people, I was to understand, were out there, unaware of forces and desires, of wills that wished to help them or mold and shape them. Yet this kind of talk about politics had a peculiar tone to it. Surely its roots were in the common meanings linking word to word, like all speech I had heard, but it lacked the twisted complexities of fear, of childish greed, of arrogance and inspiration. This political stuff had a disembodied quality to it; one spoke or read it as though its very roots in a human being had been nipped or, at the very least, skillfully disguised.

What Arthur read, what he and his friends spoke about, was meant to place me, a passive listener, in history with a nation, a class, all of which were anything but personal for me. Instead, I was hearing the myriad shufflings of ants, the dry scratchings of locusts' wings, death rattles of the personal. I developed a distaste for these papery atonalities, for their abstractness or, worse, their attenuated passion.

But this schematic, jargon-laden verbiage was not the only "political" language that I was hearing from Arthur. In 1947, Miami Beach, where my family, including Arthur, lived, although predominantly Jewish, was as "lily white" as any other part of the South. The municipal government, following the laws and codes of most towns and cities in Florida, was decidedly segregationist. There was not a black person in the school nor one residing within the city limits save as a maid in some well-off person's house. It was against the law for a black person to be on Miami Beach, an island, after nine o'clock in the evening, without a photo ID obtained from the police department.

In such a social climate, Arthur, as one of the editors of the high school newspaper, courageously wrote impassioned pleas for integration. These articles burned with all of Arthur's sense of injustice; they also nearly got him suspended from school. They scared my mother, who had to go to school and defend Arthur to the principal and teachers. When I read these tracts, often quietly mumbling them to myself, I imagined Arthur angrily orating them out loud, teaching the truth and shaming a hostile crowd. Though I felt fearful for him, I secretly revelled in his indignation and championed him to my close friends. To this day, the political language that moves me is testamentary: the impassioned sonorities of witnessing as in the songs and diaries of former slaves or in Paul Celan's poetry and in the finely graded prose of Primo Levi, forms of language that retrace the abysmal and terrifying effects of a political idea.

Arthur also led me subtly, without his knowledge, toward something deeply positive and informing. Precocious and intelligent, he often came at night to the bedroom I shared with my sister Tena to read portions of the *Iliad* to us. Arthur's voice was high-pitched and nasal; when he read quickly, it too sounded a bit like a drone, albeit a persistent one. If I was sleepy and yet fighting off sleep, I felt the battle for Troy occurring on the

MY COUSIN ARTHUR who lived with us in Miami Beach. His reading aloud of poetry to me "led me subtly, without his knowledge, toward something deeply positive and informing."

borders of my consciousness, itself a vast dark plain like the one before that ancient city. As my attention flagged, the story and the war would bleed into the black sky with its faint stars that rimmed the edge of my mind. But, if I had been sent to bed too early and was wide awake, my mind would register in full detail the horrific story of war and destruction, the mad arbitrary killing of the twelve Trojan youths by Achilles or the constant dragging of corpses behind chariots, for example, such things which in their wanton cruelty would impress themselves on a child's mind.

What I now associate with poetry, though then it was inarticulate, was the incredible suspense when Arthur read the seemingly endless chapter enumerating the order of battle for the Athenian army. All the foreign names and places, substantive upon substantive, noun upon noun, piled up like a towering wall of bricks awaiting that one verb to be uttered: "struggle" or "conflict" or "battle." I imagined this word to be like the shot from a starter's pistol, a miracle word which would trigger the entire verbal edifice into catastrophic motion, thus creating War itself. This, for me, was the magic of poetry—as opposed to story telling—that it came down finally to a word (or to the word that a poem was) which produced this forceful transformation, this flood of all the words and rhythms that had come before it. The strength of the accretory passages in the Homeric epic, and more familiarly, the great parallel lines of the Biblical narratives with their whiplike curling snaps were anticipations of an ultimate deliverance that resided in some cosmic final word, a word that would stop time in its tracks and arrest death. As a child, I understood this as a power of words, not yet as a terminology.

There was a sober, less magical side to my sense of poetry as well. It came, as I now recall, with my first conscious memory of poetry *as poetry*. This was in my early teens some years after my family had moved to South Florida because of my mother's ill health. My father, after disentangling himself from his New York business affairs, had managed to start up his small public relations firm. One of his friends, Henry Smith, a newspaper man, as my father had once been, regularly visited the house on Sunday afternoons. Smith was not his real name, for he had had one of those gutteral Polish-Jewish last names which must have caused him great difficulty in the mainly non-Jewish newspaper business. Smith was a sad-faced man, with dark baggy surfaces under his eyes, probably from drinking. It was rare that he arrived at the house without the smell of strong liquor on his breath. He never showed signs of being even mildly inebriated, but rather displayed a palpable reserve. Everything about him seemed committed to self-containment, even the tie and jacket which he wore on the most casual of occasions, such as a picnic or a visit to the beach with my family. Smith suffered from epilepsy, and there was a story that his wife had left him because she could not bear the tension of wondering when his next attack would come and then waiting to see if he would survive it. Perhaps Smith himself could not bear this tension and expressed the imminence of his death by dressing as though already laid out as a corpse.

Smith liked to slick back his thinning hair in the style of an oldtime movie actor. The hair and the underlying pallor of his face, its bulbous nose, concentrated one's image of the man above the Adam's apple. What one noticed when he called at the house of an evening or a Sunday was the marginality of his figure. When he entered, it was as though a leaf, dry and autumnal, had blown under the door.

Smith seemed to hold his thoughts tight to himself, like an old bathrobe around a frail body. Every reminder of him, from his often askew bow tie, the misplaced formality of his dress, bespoke the pain of existence, the surety of defeat. He was clever in the way some people are who do not wish to laugh, using dry wit to undercut any enthusiasm or robustness.

My father, by contrast, loved a good joke, took people at face value and was enthusiastic to the point of getting himself mixed up in some fantastic or slightly shady schemes. In the Twenties, he'd tried to make movies in Tampa, hiring major league baseball players as stars, had sold some Florida real estate during the Boom that was half swamp and half underwater. He had practiced law in New York, dabbled in politics, and had it not been for some youthful delicacy to his mental constitution, he could easily have fallen in with the city's clubhouse hacks and schmoozers. Much later, after I had grown up and moved away, he was still looking for some "big" deal which would put the family in the black. After the first successful American space flights took place, he created a business called the Galactic Interplanetary Board of Trade which sought out the endorsements of astronauts for various consumer products such as toothpaste and deodorant. Cleaning out his office after he died, I discovered a big handpress seal used for embossing letters and memos with the letters "G.I.B.O.T.," the acronym for the firm. The seal fooled no one; indeed, pressed into a piece of writing paper, it reminded me of the "official" look of much junk mail. At one time, the rumor went, my father had been a middleman in selling Canadian jet planes to pre-Castro Cuba. I knew that he had an advertising account with the Cuban pineapple industry and travelled often to Havana and Camaguey, but the idea of my father consciously involved in international skullduggery struck me as faintly ludicrous. As I sensed it, my father was basically a *naïf*, too complicit and certainly too trusting in his business deals. More often than not he would lose money on his schemes or be fleeced by the sharks he had mistaken for friends who swam in the quasi-legal waters around him.

My father had always considered himself a bit of a wordsmith. When, as a young man, he had worked as a reporter on *The Brooklyn Eagle*, he was quite proud of the fact that he had once written copy alongside reporters such as Walter Winchell and Earl Wilson. As a publicist and sometime political campaign manager in Florida, he daily ground out press releases, news reports, and political oratory for his campaigning clients. Writing had been an essential element in his marriage. He loved my mother deeply, and living in New York, apart from her when her first convalescences in Miami Beach began, he expressed his love, writing her two or three letters a day, often including short, trite love poems he had composed.

My father had watched without complaint while my mother's heart trouble, and the many complications that besieged her, wreaked havoc in the family. Not only did it force unwanted and painful separations on us, but it resulted in my father spending whatever money he made, a small fortune over the years, on her medical bills, losing all chance of making a financial killing. Indeed, my parents died penniless; we children paid the funeral costs and reimbursed the creditors.

All my father's missed or dashed business chances had their effect on him. As with Smith, life had tunneled him with subterranean sadnesses, deeps and concavities of disappointment, which displayed themselves only in his most unguarded moments. In the evening, I might momentarily espy him sitting in his armchair looking off out a window, an unglanced-at newspaper on his lap. "Michael," he would say, if I tried to engage him, "I have no time for fun now." His usually animated face would be slack, his eyes sallow and bloodshot. Seeing him thus, in a house where at times, because of my mother's illness, one calamitous hour might follow upon another, I would be riven with a painful sense of insecurity. In the early years of his move to Florida, when he could barely establish himself in business and when my mother's heart was particularly troublesome, I felt I was suffocating in an atmosphere without oxygen, suffused instead with the acidic smotherings of predicament and crisis.

My father covered the pain of his lost and sometimes less than exemplary life with the jolly sarcasm of a salesman or bunco artist, a quality that was part of his complex makeup. In his social deportment and indeed in the depths of his character, my father was poetic-sentimental or sentimental-poetic. He was not only a soft touch for beggars and poor friends, but seemed to gather around him an entourage of life's small losers. Out of work New Yorkers—people who smiled in ellipses of broken, discolored teeth, whose shirts and dresses, frayed and spotted and smelling of sweat and suntan oil—these could be found holding court daily in our Miami Beach living room. Since my mother was sick, they thoughtfully, without wishing to disturb her, helped themselves to the contents of our liquor cabinets and refrigerator. My father did not know how to say no these guests, and thus spent much of his time fixing their parking tickets and finding pick-up work or leafletting jobs for his charges. I believe he befriended Henry Smith at least in part because Smith had no other friends.

On their Sunday visits, Smith and my father suddenly transformed themselves into European gentlemen. Courtly in their manner, they sat with a bottle of schnapps and glasses in our little living room, listening to music and reading poetry to each other out of a big red omnibus anthology of world poetry. These occasions enabled the two men, despite their different styles, to signal and communicate to each other their own inner wars with sentiment.

My father's likes in music and poetry were merely another branching of his character. When home, he hummed schmaltz such as "Golden Earrings," "The Girl of My Dreams," and the like. His classical tastes rarely strayed from the sudsy, florid regions of Tchaikovsky and Rachmaninoff. Poetry for him was the booming set pieces such as "Hiawatha" or "The Charge of the Light Brigade" or various romantic love poems which have long since slid into oblivion. He read these poems with what I thought was an unseemly drama, with a kind of coarse emphasis, his voice thudding on plaintive words like *love* or *hope*. Occasionally something sardonic would rise up from his unconscious, and if I were in the living room, he would lean over, putting his face close, eyes looking malevolently into mine but with a giveaway smile on his lips, stage whispering "The BOY stood ON the BUR-Ning DECK . . ."

Smith had a more astringent taste in poetry, another clue to me that he led an unhappy life. His stoical nature, it seemed, made him a more elegant reciter of poems. Each verse was uttered with the utmost severity and circumspection, as though the words were being pitched down into the depths of his troubled life, there to be tested against Smith's own personal fate. When Smith recited a poem, there was a throttled-down energy in his voice and little white balls of spittle would form on his lips. I thought this presaged an attack of the epilepsy and would have to turn my eyes away or shut them tight.

Smith mostly chose to read poems by Hardy or Frost or E. A. Robinson, poems that depicted humanity in its minor or embittered key while emphasizing what was fatalistic: the natural world's crushing inevitablity or the outsized nature of guilt and greed. If my father's recitations often sounded fatuous or absurd, Smith's were quietly electrifying, even scary. At times, the words pierced so close to the bone, it seemed he was reciting poetry with the lips of his own deathmask. While Smith read, my father nodded rhythmically and occasionally clucked his tongue, a ripple of agitation crossing his face. Smith, it was plain, was not playing at cultural appreciation but reading existentially. It was typical of my father to skirt the unpleasantness of deep feeling, to "make nice" as my mother used to comment dryly. it was a habit of years, keeping children's fears at bay or waving away the hovering black wings of financial ruin. My father referred to Smith as "silver tongued," but in this, as in many other things, my father was being sentimental.

One Sunday, after their readings concluded, Smith went off to the newspaper, the *Florida Sun,* which had its offices only a few blocks from our house. About two o'olock in the morning, the night watchman called my father to tell him that Smith was dead, slumped over his desk. Smith had had a seizure while working late and had choked on his own tongue with no one to hear him. My father, the only person acknowledged to have more than a business relationship with Smith, was the first to be called. When I heard the news about his death, I hoped someone had wiped his lips before too many people had gathered.

Looking back, I see that Smith's asperities, his dry intonings of Hardy's "Neutral Tones" or Frost's "The Woodpile," were a significant part of the formative overhearings of my childhood, a necessary understanding to my growing up. Mankind had many quarrels with God; even its unbelievers wrung their hands and hectored and complained. My father obscured his own such quarrels with sentimental glosses, jokes, and caricatures. For obscuring and sentimentalizing were, of course, in the very essence of Miami Beach, the hotel lobbies of which, with their ornate clusters of furniture borrowed easily from French Provincial to chinoiserie, were meant to lull the tourist into false associations with wealth and taste and high culture.

Smith, it struck me, had lived without the sheen. His circumspect recitations of tragic poetry revealed not only that poetry's burden of truth, but also its authentic rasp. He was its perfect instrument, sounding a measured elegance amidst all those vain scratchings on the glassy wall of God's invisibility. His voice remains audible to me as the record of someone who oriented himself toward fate with economy and precision.

II

CHILDREN love disasters and wars, provided they are sufficiently distant and that death has not yet intruded on one's family. In this passion, I was no different from either my playmates or my times.

I remember the fascination and even awe-filled delight with which, as a child, while we were still living in New York, I pored over the newspaper clippings of 1942 that my parents had saved of the burning ocean liner *Normandie* tipped on its side at its pier in New York Harbor. There had been speculation in the newspapers that the fires on the *Normandie* had been set by saboteurs and foreign agents. Only months before, the destruction of Europe had already begun.

I recall, years later, my mother telling me how, almost immediately after the radio broadcast the news of the fire, she and my father, as though possessed by feelings they could not account for, had bundled me up, a mere babe, and driven along the West Side Highway past the burning ship to see for themselves what the disaster was like. My mother's recollections were given to me in a voice both muted and contrite, an embarrassed confession. I wondered, had this handsome middle-aged couple held me, a small child of five, to the window to look out on that burning wreckage; had they, too, succumbed to the disaster-fever of those years?

Naturally, I remember nothing of that drive. My impressions of the burning ship came a bit later from the newsphotos my parents saved, from bound volumes of photographs collected from the pages of *Life* and *Time*. These photos absorbed me with their granular renderings of the smoke and steam which enshrouded the white painted bridge and superstructure of the ship as it lay half submerged in the water alongside the Hudson River dock. I would lean down close to where the pictures lay on the table top as though I might be able to peek under the venting steam. For beneath those billowing clouds blown white across those spread open pages, one could make out minute harried beings clinging and scurrying on board the burning vessel and at dockside. What looked like oily black smoke and flame spewed up from the decking. Mysterious metallic torques revealed themselves in the odd swerves and bent tracks of rivet-heads along the buckling plates. Symmetry itself seemed under attack as, with my magnifying glass, I peered at the goose bumps of heat-blistered paint. The grain of the photographs, the clusters of oddly shaded dots, which I studied, trying to see the faces of those few crewmen still on board, was a map of the incommensurable, a child's pointillist quantum—a blur up close, but resolving itself, as one moved back, into a portrait, curiously more comforting, of chaos and misfortune.

I was looking at these photos in the midst of the Second World War, when catastrophe was already becoming the yeast of childhood. It bubbled up through the sedate end of our block in Brooklyn's Bedford Stuyvesant section with its scrap drives and bandage rolling parties. It filled rooms with the fetid aroma of jar after jar of fat sitting on the kitchen window sill above the sink waiting to be collected and trucked to munitions plants and chemical factories. The beasts of death, the metallic stores of our armories and arsenals, the weapons bathed in cosmoline, the foul exhausts of tanks, indeed murder and carnage themselves, must smell like this, I thought.

Catastrophe fluoresced over the dull pages of the grade school history books. It gave immediacy to the way my first grade classmates and I divvied up into armies after school in the play yard: Germans versus Americans, Germans versus British, Germans versus French, Germans versus anything. The *Shoah*, the purgatorial apostrophe of European Jewish life, was barely a rumor among the then mostly Jewish families of Bedford Stuyvesant. That terrible occurrence was a vague disturbance in the communications machinery far offshore, a slight vibratory *ping*, muted and orchestrated by politicians and the newspapers. As such, no one could yet imagine the configuration of that horrific oblivion to come. Children were most unaware of it except perhaps as a heightened nervousness among grownups, as if the sluggish body of American Jewry were experiencing in the form of mild galvanic shocks the vitriol of Hitler and his followers.

For us children, then, the Germans were classified merely as "the bad guys," on a par with the American Indians or outlaw gangs of the Westerns; to be a "German" in our games was as much fun as being an "American."

After we were let out of class, our little wars continued in the deserted ruins of the Ruppert Brewery across from the school. Its half-demolished smokestacks and brick archways, rubble-strewn hallways, its stacks of tarred lumber and plaster-coated lathing reeked with adult destruction, with sanctioned malevolence. Here our stick rifles poked around dizzying ambuscades of tile and rusted iron, every scrap heap an enemy ambush or heroically defended hill.

Being caught and being play-shot, one had to lie down, eyes closed, on the rubble-littered ground for a count of fifty; it was one of our strictest rules. Since the others went on screaming and shouting around one, this lying prone in the dirt produced an irrepressible tension in every nerve end and every heartbeat. It threatened to throw one erect and was, in the moment, the cruellest of all childhood tortures. Yet to leap up was to risk being ejected from the game, to risk going home long before dinner was ready or to slink like an outcast along the streets in the deepening and somehow melancholy shadows of buildings.

The adrenaline rushes of our war games, which pulsed with the same jagged rhythms of the news, made us feel doubly alive. They seemed dictated not by us but by some conspiracy of the century, as if the old men, the war-mongering fathers of our history primers and fairy tales, the bearded states-men and dead kings—and being dead meant only that one had to count to fifty before rising again—had infused the air with this disaster taste.

My interest in science and engineering must have begun in those dark and blighted years. War and catastrophes involved technology and equipment, much of which partook of that strange discordant music of civilization playing itself out before one's eyes, of things being built up and then toppled. Machinery of all sorts, particularly that built on a grand scale, immediately possessed my own and my playmates' minds. Complicated structures with rows of iron bolts, with cross-hatched girders, swinging cranes, things that moved in odd, nonhuman ways with slow gestures as though scribing ruled lines or arcs on the sky, these would totally absorb me.

Many of my earliest play drawings were crude renderings of machines, quick sketches, penned-in inkblots of this metallurgical *Zeitgeist*. I was more adept at drawing a railroad bridge, where I would labor over every rivet and railroad tie, than I was at drawing the human figure or face. I would show these to my parents. My mother was always quick to praise, but my father would give them only a cursory glance and put them aside. He had no interest that I know of in things mechanical, nothing of the craftsman or tinkerer in him. The photo albums of my memory bank hold no images of him leaning under car hoods or doing carpentry in the basement. While my boyhood friends talked about their fathers fixing this or making that, I was struck by my father's indifference to this entire side of existence. I can't remember him so much as picking up a hammer or wrench.

Nor do I recall that he knew much of the technical side of Rosenthal Brothers, the firm he and my mother's brother Sam (Arthur's father, who died young) had inherited from my mother's family. This business, taking up a high floor in an old loft building on Lower Broadway, made trimmings, tassels, and curtain cords. One took a creaking old elevator up to the loft and immediately stepped into a long narrow room filled with a mass of spinning machinery where hundreds of whirling spindles fed threads into rows of weaving machines at one end, and where bright multicolored cord poured out of the other onto oversized spools. The spools were wound with strands of green and red thread, with garish oranges and yellows, or with gleaming threads of gold lamé in varying combinations. The lamé was Rosenthal Brothers' finest, most delicate product; the least bit of rough handling would crack the surface of the thread and produce a little snowfall of golden flakes. The machine on which this thread was woven, with gold clinging to all its surfaces, looked positively Egyptian.

In the loft, Manny and Solly, my father's two younger, cigar-smoking Italian business partners and foremen, would flit up and down the aisles between the machinery like a pair of acrobatic clowns, changing spools and spindles, splicing threads and untangling jam-ups. At times they clambered up into the machinery, pulling themselves along on the brass knobs and blackened rods; there they hung head down, unravelling knots or yanking great tangles of thread out of the clattering machines. They whistled, talked, joked, their feet kicking the air above them, their heads nearly touching the floor. They appeared to be performing an extraordinary modern ballet, even more interesting than the marching and wheeling toy soldiers in *The Nutcracker* that I saw at Carnegie Hall each Christmas while we still lived in New York.

When they weren't working, the two young partners came over and entertained me with jokes or funny magic tricks. Manny, handsome and well built, and with a pencil moustache, knew how to make coins appear and disappear, and Solly, short and rounded with baby fat, could pull his face and nose out of shape with his fingers. I fell to the floor holding my sides and laughing.

My father preferred staying in the front of the loft where the offices were located. How strange he looked there, dressed in his suit, his white starched shirt, and tie, and, as I think of it now, a bit stranded in his middle age. He had led a wild, adventurous youth, but now, as I look back, struck a figure that was not only older but seemed to have grown backward in time as well. He sat in the front office, occasionally calling back inquiries but mostly spending time on the phone or dictating letters to his secretary above the loud humming of the machines. Here, like an anachronism from another, more innocent time, my father presided over the declining fortunes of Rosenthal Brothers. The yearly trial balances worked up by Mr. Schlossberg, an accountant from the neighborhood, showed one series of losses after another. The cause may have been the shifting of tastes and fashions consequent on the war years or simply my father's poor handling of money matters. Or perhaps the losses were more indicative of the slow passing of a way of life in which, among other things, heavy brocaded drapes were pulled each evening, as though securely encircling families and even whole continents from each other.

The business failures, as I see them now, were representative of my father's essentially romantic and sentimental nature, a nature that was profoundly blunted on the new demands of rationality and calculation that more and more were to make up the iron law of the world.

Often, when I was at the loft, I sat, somewhat precariously, on the ledge of a big open window and played with a little magnetized monkey that hopped up and down a metal pole. There was a foot-high lip of stone on the ledge, enough I suppose my father thought, to keep me from falling into the shimmering, snakelike, traffic-jammed depths of Lower Broadway. From beneath me rose the sound of traffic of the street, the grinding of truck gears and the honking of horns; behind me was the incessant whirr and clacking of the spinning machines. When concentration on my little toy lapsed, I suddenly became aware of where I was, of my perch on that precarious bit of stone, and of being pressed between these two vast sheets of noise. The sounds seemed to bear me up and hold me frozen to the window ledge, but were, as well, striated with the time's ominous and strident deliriums that threatened to throw me down into the street.

I remember how my family's drawn expressions as we sat around listening to FDR's speech the night of Pearl Harbor both scared and infuriated me. I wanted to shout, if only to release the moment. But my brother Bummy's ashen face—he was twelve, eight years older—frightened the wits out me. The war's distant yet violent commotions and the uncertainties surrounding me came closer, reinforced by events actually taking place in our household.

One of these occurrences had been my father's enlisting in the National Guard. In the late nineteen thirties, he had signed up with the New York State Guard as a kind of sociopolitical lark, giving him a chance to play soldier and to hang around for a couple of weeks each year with his clubhouse buddies, the backroom lawyers and municipal judges of Brooklyn civic culture. And now, in those early days and months of the Second World War, my father completed Non-commissioned Officers Training School and received a commission on June 17th, 1942, as a Second Lieutenant in Brooklyn's 13th Regiment. The various letters giving this information were all on official forms, the sentences routinely reproduced in faded brown ink which made up the body of the letter. My father's name, as though an afterthought, was typed in in a fresh, stronger, black ink following the brown "Dear" of the salutation. There his name lay at the top of those letters like a spare part for a machine sitting on a warehouse shelf.

I accounted my father some kind of warrior even though he was nearly forty, and so, instead of going into combat overseas, was sent away for a few weeks at a time to Camp Smith in Plattsburgh to train younger men to fight. On the days on which he went off, he put on his dress khakis, and having a slim and elegant carriage, and with a thin leather belt across his chest, he no longer resembled the slightly lost man in the offices of Rosenthal Brothers but looked instead like a picture book hero. No sooner had his car pulled away from our house, than my older brother Bummy started to chase my younger sister Tena and me through our large brownstone on Pulaski Street, waving old bazooka shells and hollowed-out training grenades, a malevolent treasure hoard brought back by my father from Camp Smith. Often, Bummy pursued us into the backyard. Like harbingers of the war, gypsy moths had invaded Brooklyn that summer of 1942, and we ran laughing and screaming under trees stripped of leaves and bearing, like war wounds, the stumps of amputated branches.

Yet a number of things concerning the war affected me in a more sobering way. One was the air raid drills with their solemn rituals of drawn

HEADQUARTERS SECOND SERVICE COMMAND TACTICAL SCHOOL
Camp SCd-4, Hackettstown, New Jersey

December 10, 1942

2nd Lieutenant Peter F. Heller, NYSG,
13th Regiment,
Brooklyn, N. Y.

My dear Lieutenant Heller:

I am happy to learn that you will be in attendance at the coming session of the Second Service Command Tactical School. We hope to make your tour of duty here a profitable and pleasant experience.

There is inclosed herewith an instruction sheet and a train and bus schedule which will aid you in making your preparation for arrival. It is recommend   you be prepared for cold weather. The camp is located in mou   ous country and crisp Fall weather may be expected.

It is requested that you report on arrival at the Supply Building for processing. It is planned to conduct processing between 3 P. M. and 5 P. M. on the opening day of each school course and while it is requested that you report no later than 5 P. M., it would be desirable if you would report earlier.

Awaiting your arrival, I am

2-Incls.
    Instruction Sheet
    Train & Bus Schedule

Cordially yours,

HARLAN BESSON
Lieut. Colonel, Infantry
Commandant

LETTER inviting my father to Command Tactical School, 1942. His name lay at the top of the letter "like a spare part for a machine."

blackout curtains and wailing sirens that seemed to cut the house off from the rest of the world. I was, childishly, angered by them too, especially because of the isolation they imposed. The great thing about my school-yard play-disasters was that one went through them with companions. Here, there were no friends, only the bed and the empty halls and rooms of the house awash in the darkness. Everywhere, the heavy damask curtains swallowed up one's vision. As one gazed upon the dull, nonreflecting textures of the cloth, the universe appeared to contract, suffocatingly, to

MY FATHER on bivouac at Camp Smith, Plattsburgh, N.Y., 1943.

the walled chamber one stood in. When the sirens began, one's room, even one's entire house and family, floated off like a spore into that blackened world outside bent on self-wreckage. As though anchorless and rudderless, one felt a sense of being cast off, of drifting, detached and vulnerable. Aloneness struck one to the roots.

My own need for solitude when I am writing, and which is vestigial in character, stems, I think, from this time. To this day, a dark amorphous night, an undifferentiated "outside," can arouse in me an irrational surge of fear. I have experienced it in the mountains when clouds loom or the moon is blocked. I've been touched with terror where trees hide houses and sky. This fear is not without pleasure, for I have often conceived the urge to write as the setting down of a word in the blankness of space, as the dropping of an anchor in the abyss. As a writer, I have tried to summon or trick out that abyss or uncertainty, to make my own being depend, finally, on a word. In this condition, another person's presence would only contaminate the situation with the familiar.

There were, then, those ambivalent moments of the war years, when my father was away at the training camp, in which the real nature of events crept in: fear, loss, the few gold stars in windows down the block marking those families whose men had been killed in the war. Such things settled on my chest suffusing me with both fear and self-definition as I fell into troubling sleeps.

It was also during this period—I was four and going on five years of age—that I became aware of my mother's heart trouble. As a young girl, she had developed rheumatic fever; now, in her thirties, beneath her warm and soft bosom, her heart valves skipped irregularly. She complained of pain shooting down her arms and into her finger tips.

Doctors were regularly summoned to the house, and we all gathered at the door as they entered, the entire household parting like the Red Sea before Moses. These doctors, it must be remembered, were perceived as being at the very peak of the evolutionary possibilities of Jewish middle-class life. Never mind the *zaddiks* and scholars lost in their bookishness and as bound to poverty as a donkey to its cart. A doctor's learning, by all respectable accounts, was alchemical, turning book knowledge into useable gold and even on occasion, gentile respect. And so what airs these gentlemen had. They preened; they reproduced mannerisms like wind-up toy men; in place of words, their voices piped out "tuts" and low-keyed "hmmms." They could have been a new species of bird, part penguin and part vulture. Dr. Nishman, for instance, who lived only next door, always arrived wearing a checkered weskit, his neck powdered and his short corpulent presence aromatic with barbershop lotions and oils. From the pocket of the weskit dangled a gold fob, the very center of his *gravitas*. He often played with it when discussing my mother's illness. One's eye followed the rhythms of the fob as much as one's ears followed the words he uttered. Was the fob making small erratic circles or was it whirring through the air like a propeller? Somehow its motions seemed a better indicator of my mother's condition than the toy steam whistles, the *ahmms*, or the locutions and evasions of his speech. Dr. Nishman's coming to the house almost always signalled something far too serious to be neighborly, and left, in the wake of his visits, a positively medical and ornithological confusion.

This calamity of my mother's health was an entirely different affair from the distant wars outside. For one thing, it was surrounded by frequent panic and commotion on the part of our entire family, friends and relatives; it was "adult," in other words. It reduced us children to mere terrified automatons, who were to wait in each crisis of my mother's illness to do exactly as we were told lest any mischance on our part produce a terrible disaster.

When very ill, my mother was ordered to remain in bed, my parent's bedroom being a long room on the second or parlor floor of the house, with a bay window overlooking the street at one end and a dark cramped library at the other. On certain days, usually after a night of alarums and rushings about, from which we were tyrannically excluded by the adults, when it seemed like the entire sky would fall in on us, my sister, the youngest, and I were forbidden to come within thirty feet of my mother's bed. We were, however, allowed to stand in the dark shadows of the library and to look along the polished wood floors to where my mother's bed stood like some sacrificial altar, replete with flowers and drapery. Had I known the word *infinity* its cognate would have been that untransversable stretch of parallel boards that ran from us to her.

On certain days, it seemed that my mother, in that bed, barely moved, and indeed, the thought that she was really dead flitted across my mind. The light pouring through the windows often gave to her end of the room a churchlike, funereal appearance, as though the hand of the deity had descended on the light beams to raise her up. The trees across the street, which threw their dark, mottled shadows against the windows and across her bedcovers, were closer to my mother than I was allowed to come.

As my mother's episodes of illness continued, the doctors were again and again consulted, and even roused out in the night to come and stamp through the house yelling orders to hired nurses and telling us to shut up and go back to our rooms. The entire family plunged into a daily fearful despair.

With me, this despair took the form of being especially concerned about the exact location of my mother's presence. Was she behind me or above me, perhaps in the kitchen or pantry or by the dining room tables somewhere or on that second floor of book-lined shelves and endless sinister vistas along narrow floorboards which I had been prohibited to cross?

And yet I knew that she was there in one of these places, the back of the house or her room, even as I sat in the front parlor in the late winter afternoon surrounded by the immense shapes of our overstuffed furniture and listened to the mystery stories crackling out of the speaker of the radio. This radio, one of those large mahogany floor models, had a green tuning eye about the size of a half dollar, and in the darkened room, it bulked there almost as another living thing, gazing with its eerie beam into the shadows. There, pressed into the cushions of the sofa, I easily migrated into the make-believe stories of afternoon radio, the thrillers and ghost tales, as though arriving at another country. The green light functioned for me something like a lighthouse; I was a sailor approaching the edge of a shore made up of entangling sound forms and narratives, and they, these crisscrossed pathways of words and stories, were places, deserted islands or lost continents, where I could lose track of myself and my worries. As lost in the radio broadcasts as I might get, the light also reminded me that I was in the same house, near my mother who was everything: warmth, shelter, responsiveness.

Toward the end of 1943, my mother, who had been a school teacher, retired with a disability pension from the New York City Board of Education. About that time, a letter from my father to his Commanding Officer in the 13th Regiment requested a leave of absence to take my mother to a "convalescent home."

It was in this context that the words "California," "Florida," and "Miami Beach" began to be heard around the house. They were uttered by parents and relatives in long-faced discussions with the doctors and relatives, and with my father's business partners, Manny and Solly. Each place word came freighted with merits and demerits, and aroused champions and detractors who argued long into the night. From my bedroom, I could hear faintly, the strained voices, the heated weighting of climates and geographies, the fearsome debates over the percentage of Jews in the populace. Nor did my mother participate in these deliberations; she retired early as well, to lay immured, I am sure, in semi-darkness on her bed.

Suddenly, my father was bringing home brightly colored travel brochures, train schedules, and newspapers such as *The Miami Herald* and *The Florida Sun*. Over the course of several weeks, these were nightly splayed across the dining table for the family conferees to finger and inspect. The dining room light centered over the table cast a large yellowish oval across these pieces of paper as they were discussed and passed about. The shiny brochures caught the light and sent little beams out into the corners of the room to where we, the children, were banished.

In my memory, these dining room scenes, like those de la Tour paintings of the eighteenth century that are drenched in candlelight, fix adult and child in tableaux of anguish, fear, and powerlessness. For it seemed, at the time, there was no longer any patience for us left in the house. When we timidly approached close to find out what was being discussed, shouts warned us away. An air of hysteria had been created, and it could have been war strategy or an autopsy which was being performed on that table.

Solly, who was my best adult friend in the world, could see our confusion and distress. Now and then, he'd turn to my sister and me, light a cigarette, and with a crazy cross-eyed expression on his face, he'd swallow the burning cigarette whole and blow smoke out of his ears. Then, in mock astonishment, he'd pluck the cigarette from his right ear, look at it hungrily and swallow it again. Unable to control ourselves, laughing and tittering, we would creep up to the table beside him. Manny would poke Solly in the ribs, telling him to cut it out, and again, my father and the others would erupt into a hail of shouts, and back we scurried to the edges of the room.

Then, one day it was clear that something had been decided. Dr. Nishman arrived at the house, perfumed sartorial feathers and all, the bright weskit and gleaming fob bouncing gently on his pot belly, to announce in stentorian tones something we all knew, that my mother would be moved to Florida within a few weeks, and that shortly the rest of the family could follow. My father immediately pulled us aside to tell us that eventually we would all be going to Florida to live with my mother. It was part of the plan, my father told us, to bit by bit resettle the entire family on Miami Beach.

I cannot remember the exact day of my mother's first departure for Florida. I do remember her giving us each a kiss at the door of 172 Pulaski Street and being driven off in my father's two-toned blue Oldsmobile. It was 1943, the second year of the war, blackness, siren-filled nights, and her disappearance plunged the gloomy basement living room and kitchen of that flaking brownstone into an even darker vacuum.

The anguish of separation affected my nerves which, like a dead frog's, had been given a galvanic response. I suddenly began to twitch all over; my body broke out in rashes. The dark living room, with the blatting one-eyed radio, the shadowy slopes and valleys of upholstery, became again a moonscape of frights. Was my mother truly to be lost to me? Days for children are like weeks; months closer to centuries than years.

Now, in troubled fantastical dreams, my mother became a historical figure, a player from some adult costume drama who appeared nightly but with a sense of foreboding and forlorness, and I lived with the memory of her as I did with the vaguer memories of storybooks and fables. She had become one of those anguished spirits of the night that seemed to visit me only in sleep and then only to hector me over my faults, which had made her desert me in the first place.

In the family scrapbooks, there is a postcard written by my father in May 1943, mailed from Fort Pierce, Florida enroute back to New York and addressed to my mother at the Arlington Hotel, Ocean Drive and Fifth Street, Miami Beach. The postcard is a tinted and retouched photograph of Miami Beach's Lincoln Road. In it, the sky is a pale, inviting blue, and the buildings are all captured in creamy white perfection, their colorful but dignified awnings giving the place a stately air. The automobiles, mostly black and glistening in the sun, suggest beetles marching in regular columns along the paving. Possibly the postcard records a short scouting mission on my parents' part, for in May of 1944, my father again requested a leave of absence from his CO to take my mother to Florida. In any case, by early-1944, my mother was living at the Hudson Arms on 15th Street in Miami Beach, and I was scheduled to go down there for a

POSTCARD of Miami Beach from the early nineteen forties. "The automobiles, mostly black and glistening in the sun, suggest beetles . . ."

lengthy visit during the spring half of the school year. This card, which I saw on my mother's dresser on this, my initial visit to Florida, is now burnt into my mind as one of the first places by which she could be located. It constitutes an ideality, a memory against which the subsequent reality of Miami Beach was to be held and found wanting.

My father, being too involved in his business matters to make the trip himself, turned me over to the Schusterhoffs, another Brooklyn family, distant relatives it turned out, whom he asked to bring me with them on the train and deliver me to my mother. Of that train ride I remember little of the scenery except the pine forests and savannahs of the Carolinas and Georgia, the irregular rows of the trees and the great swampy flats that seemed to embody the longing for my mother that I felt. Much more vivid in my memory was the heaviness of the plated silverware in the dining car, the creamers and sugar bowls lustered and bright, the interiors of which blossomed an egg-colored gold. They were the very symbols of solidity and respectability. Like my mother's silver and cut glass, they stood as minute bulwarks of self-definition against the changes that were to come. To me, they looked curiously perfect as though embodying the weightiness of lives, something that, in the marbled black hands of the white-coated porters, would last forever.

The train arrived in the middle of a sleepy morning in downtown Miami, which at that time was—once one was away from the waterfront areas—very much a Southern town of small houses, hibiscus bushes and palms. From the station, empty, untrafficked streets marched off in grid square patterns walled in by spanish tile and rain-streaked stucco, a few scrawny palms and fruit trees shimmering in the heat. Far off, two lonely-looking high rise buildings, rather simplified in design and constituting Miami's downtown, stood desolately in the withering sunlight. This was not "Florida" as I had understood it from my mother's postcards showing canals and cool white buildings set in lush tropical foliage. Possibly, this was only the "South" which had been timidly discussed and deplored at dinner times when the plans for my mother's new home were being made.

Indeed, now that I recall the hesitancies, the nearly moral character of my parent's indecisions, Florida or California, communicated to me as they can only be communicated to a child, I understood that there was something not quite right with Florida because one had to "go South" to get there. And this station was, even at a glance, redolent of that South, tinged for my parents by a faint immorality, with its segregated facilities, its black people in uniforms or old clothes with their mock deferentiality and politeness. The black soldiers—this was during World War II—could be seen filing off the far end cars of the train, to huddle only for moments and then disperse from the station. It was as though, having experienced things a little bit differently in the north or in the Army camps, they were now embarrassed and uncertain in resuming the racial pecking order of the station. As a child, I smelled the southern ethos here first as the rank sweat of poor food and hard work laced with the biting acid of resentment, soured in itself by self-containment and lack of release. Coupled with this smell was the sense that trains always arrived at odd off-hours, at times when only black people were around, who were destined to be bidden and to do the toting. I was to return to that station many times both to come to and to go from Miami, to watch across its polished floor, clumps of Jews from the north like myself, ordering the porters around, uneasily at first, then with sharpness.

By noon, the Schusterhoffs and I were in a taxi heading for their hotel on Miami Beach, leaving the dingy "South" behind us by crossing, it seemed, an endless causeway of bridges and islets, of purifying blue-green water which surrounded bright sunlit villas and sails under a deep blue sky. There was barely a cloud, as I remember; the tires ticked on the road surfaces with a clean sound, and off to my right, a giant dirigible was anchored just a few feet from the ground above trees and water. Its steel skin reflected and bent, like a funhouse mirror, the whole panorama of skies, trees, and buildings. From my seat in the taxi, I could smell the tang of salt in the air and see the dancing of miniscule dots of light caught under the sun.

At the hotel, the Schusterhoffs discovered they had misplaced my mother's address and phone number; telephone information seemed of no help and when it sunk in to me that I was not to be immediately reunited with my mother, that the Schusterhoffs would have to call my father that evening in New York, a sudden childish bitterness and depression possessed me. Paradise had been violently rent, and my mother had fallen beyond reach through its gaping hole. I burst into a tantrum, storming and crying, accusing my escorts of betrayal and stupidity. The Schusterhoffs, almost as an act of self-defense, packed their kids and me off to the beach while they tried further attempts, including calling the police, to contact my mother.

To go down to the beach, it was necessary for me to change into my bathing suit in the Schusterhoffs' hotel suite. My white skin, even paler in the dresser mirror than I imagined it, betrayed the recency of my arrival from that blackened and distant north and in my eyes exposed my newness and uncertainty, the lost ground and childhood legitimacy of place. And now, as well, entwined into my estrangement, my mother could not be found. But this shame was almost as nothing to what I felt when, a few minutes later, I emerged, thin, pale, and absurdly callow, from the lobby's swinging doors onto the sundeck with its browned bodies trussed and oiled like barbecuing chickens. Embarrassed, I ran quickly down to the sand and stood there, looking at the immense rippling planes of the ocean, the high, breaking waves of which seemed to hover over my head. I wondered what held it back from breaking over the beach, drowning the thousands who lay on their mats and blankets taking in the sun. It was then too that I had my first sight of the entire wall of hotels running up and down the island, all of them cleanly cut out of the blue of the sky, and only slightly, if fancifully, decorated with balconies and terraces.

Till then, ponds and lakes, even little streams had been my swimming holes. The ocean was what I saw from the prospect of the Coney Island boardwalk, taken there by my parents or led along though the winding streets, of Luna Park and the other amusement areas by a counsellor of my Brooklyn summer day camp. I was led to that water's edge and allowed to dip my toes, to stray up to my ankles in the roiling surf. At such times, we were careful as to how we put our wet feet in the sand lest we track up school or home. Often, we just sat on the edge of the boardwalk, our feet dangling over its edge ten feet in the air above the beach. If I remember, this was when my feet in my sneakers felt the hottest, and the thought of running down barefooted into the water was a delicious one. From the boardwalk, and even from the heights of the parachute ride and Ferris wheel, I looked out on the glittering expanse, watched the swimmers bobbing in the surf, saw the sails and the smokestacks, the shadows of clouds.

That easy motion of everything caught up in the water has always struck me as the opposite of my intense feelings of awkwardness, my gawky walk and slightly stuttering speech. Now, in the very first afternoon on the shores of Miami Beach, and with neither of my parents present, the alleviating buoyancy of the ocean was to be mine. Still, I was hesitant, for the first thing that flew into my head was that I could never swim in this, that I would be lost in its vast folds of wave and surf.

This reflection was cut short, however, when it became apparent that the bottoms of my feet were being roasted by the hot sand. I ran up to the lip of the ocean, let the tepid waters run over my feet and noticed that a sandbar stretched some distance offshore paralleling the beach as far as I could see and that other children my age were standing perhaps fifty yards offshore in water no deeper than their knees. I looked around again; the beach stretched away, blankets, people whom I had barely begun to notice, a few palms waving in the breeze, the brightly decorated hotels standing like sentinels against the sky. The whole world seemed to be witnessing this immersion of mine. I was dizzy with it and also with the heat as it fanned down from the sun. I took two steps into the water and was immediately knocked down by a breaker. Water poured into my mouth and nose as I was rolled and pounded along the bottom. I broke through to the surface for air, and found my footing. I had swallowed a good deal of salt water and as I pulled myself from the surf, feeling it suck at me from under my feet, I was leaden with the water and nauseated. I ran up the beach to the hotel.

Back in the room, the Schusterhoffs informed me that they had gotten in touch with my mother. She was on the way to the hotel to collect me.

Over the next few weeks, I met other children who told me about the German "wolf pack" submarines that had sunk ships right off the coast of Miami and left huge slicks of oil that coated the dead bodies of seaman and wreckage washing up on the beach. With those gulps I had taken of the sea, I had physically ingested a taste of the enemy, the minute and bitter savors of my childhood, the black and brackish waters of disaster.

It was also said that espionage agents were landed in the dead of night from those submarines onto American soil to spy and infiltrate. That since German and Yiddish shared many sounds in common and produced accented speech in similar ways, a Nazi agent could do worse than live among American Jews. That here, on Miami Beach, we might be break-fasting with or buying lamb chops alongside saboteurs.

When I contemplate the waves of immigrant Jews arriving at the turn of the century, the words *spying* and *infiltration* come into my mind with more complex implications. I am thinking of the Jewish experience of America and the American experience of the Jewish landfall, of thousands of *shtetl* lemmings in reverse, blindly backing out of Europe's horrors and murk, crowding into steerage. Passage across the Atlantic meant Time was unwinding, that its wound-up thread of oppressions and struggles was being unspooled toward some earlier allegorical construct of a Golden Age or Jewish Paradise. True, they were being delivered into a future, but its imagined shape was of an old Eden of peace and plenty.

For this reason, the Jews of Europe and the shores of America meet, for me, neither in the clash of cultural or religious values nor in the assim-ilations of many Jews into mainstream social and economic spheres of American life. Rather, they meet in the principle of commentary and dia-logue which undergirds so much of the thematics of Jewish thought.

The sense of commentary I am trying to invoke here involves *espying* (to spy upon and to catch sight of), to pursue and understand through close examination, as to a text, to read and decipher as the immigrant Jews had to do for themselves upon arrival. For them, the decipherment was to be of the body and text of America, the attempt to translate or decode it in terms of the mythological language of freedom and prosperity, that biblically confabulated text called America which had been given to them in the Old World.

For these disembarking immigrants, the United States was already a vast peopled landscape upon which a secret writing and telling had been inscribed. And like those fantastic seventeenth-century travel narratives (which Swift so ably parodied), this inscription was made of whispered imaginings and misheard scraps of letters sent back from the New World cities of America to the villages of Poland and Russia. This constellation of words, of hopes and fears, of multilayered internalized languages, now the psycho-physical baggage of the new arrivals, was to be—impossibly—pried out of and decoded from the harsh realities of the new ghetto-slums of New York, Philadelphia, and Boston, from the cruel labor laws or the monstrous social arrangements which configured life in another, foreign and hostile tongue.

It was into this situation that the Jews of Eastern Europe such as the members of my family infiltrated themselves. In their "code-cracking," in their commentaries on the New World, they found few points of agreement or assimilation. And yet, as with all arrivals, in all the foreignness and estrangement, in all the baffled dissonance between hope and reality, they still found niches or places on which they could stand. That is, the commentaries they created to explain this New World to themselves resembled mutual border areas, boundary markers where the otherness of America met their otherness. Their very being, the Old World narratives of village life, the prefigured America they had carried in the bellies of passenger ships and the new texts of decipherment formed both an arena of interplay and a buffer.

And in truth, no Jew owned his or her commentary: it belonged to that sprawling engarblement of language and thought, that still unfused mass of the many verbiages and word systems that constitute American life. Looked at as a multiplicity of entwined dialogues, such espying commentaries on the text of America seem like nothing so much as the work of double agents, unsure of their loyalties and possibly in the pay of both sides, Europe and America.

In my own eyes, as I think back, my father was one of the greatest of secret agents, for every layer of his being, while a true and necessary part of him, also embodied a whole CIA's worth of covers. All those professions he engaged in, from railroad worker to soldier, to film producer, lawyer, and entrepreneur, and the multitudinous "disguises" of courtier, family man, con artist, and sentimentalist, not only struck me as authentic and natural, seemly in their coexistence, but, as well, I or anyone could observe my father for hours and discover no hint of play acting or characterological duplicity.

One of the glories of these performances surely occurred in his role as a Republican in our Brooklyn ward in the late Thirties and Forties. In those days of post-Depression, New Deal sympathy and adulation for FDR, a Republican in our neighborhood of mostly working- and middle-class Jews was as rare as an albino gazelle walking down Willoughby Avenue. Herbert Hoover and his pro-business, antilabor administration represented the heights of *goyishe* chicanery and evil. Yet somehow, through a series of mysterious movements, secret desires to be a "big shot," and newly made friendships in the Brooklyn civic and courthouse culture of the Thirties, my father had not only allied himself with the Grand Old Party but had become an alternate from New York to their 1936 National Convention. He also held some minor offices in state government under Thomas E. Dewey. Indeed, a few years after my father initiated this political apostasy, Dewey befriended my father and appointed him to the state parole board, a ceremonial job requiring him to attend a few meetings a year in Albany to rubber stamp decisions made by prison officials on those convicts hoping for early release.

It was mostly routine work, but after one such trip, my father began to receive threatening phone calls. And one day, while he and my mother were at work, a man came to our home on Pulaski Street and told the maid he was our repair man. He took from the house our radios and phonograph and other appliances, said to the maid that he would also "polish the silver," and drove away with all these items in his car. When he was apprehended, after trying to fence them in the neighborhood, we learned that he was the brother of a man denied parole.

In our house, Dewey too was a kind of stolen property. Photographs of the governor, a number of them with his arm around my father, now hung over my father's desk at home. The pencil-thin moustache, the slight gap between the front teeth, the dark grey suit that, as governor of the Empire State, Dewey always wore, radiated a certain awkward if not negative power into the house. Visitors, my mother's friends in particular, peered at these photographs with a malign concentration. "Better a picture of Jesus," one of the silver-haired ladies exclaimed on seeing the beaming governor framed above my father's papers.

MY FATHER with Johnny Crews, local Republican Assemblyman, inspecting a pothole on a Brooklyn street. "A Republican in our neighborhood . . . was as rare as an albino gazelle walking down Willoughby Avenue."

But even these icons were outdone in their disorienting strangeness whenever my father put on his black silk tuxedo to go to a Republican function, a political dinner or a social event such as the Governor's Ball. Here, disguise or cover achieved an alchemical transformation, a kind of new quintessence. My father, in perfectly tailored tux and boiled shirt and with the simplest of gold studs, cuff links, and collar buttons, beclouded in the sweet but astringent aromas of aftershave lotions and hair emollients, seemed impossibly American. That is, it was not believable that he was a rabbi's son or that he lived in a Jewish middle-class ghetto of lawyers and doctors, of garment workers, butchers, and grocery store owners.

This is what I mean by my father's quintessence. For the spy must go in disguise, must yield to the language and ways of the enemy, perhaps in his or her enthusiasm going so far as to become one of them. Here then, the degree of accommodation can be seen as, also, the degree of cover, of a buried but existing difference. But accommodation also has its dark potentials, in fears or resentments, in the secret anguished desires of belonging; at any moment, these hidden differentials might break out into a strange distressed language, even into the musical texts of literature and poetry.

THE AMERICAN JEWISH CLOCK

When did Solomon (for Zalman) Heller, my grandfather, come here, his time folded into America
like honey layered in Middle-European pastry?

When did he arrive? After his pogroms and wars,
And before my father's. Was he naive? To arrive
like an autocrat, to enter like a king, in the train

of minor victories. Zalman, here called Solomon!
With a new syllable to lengthen his name. In the vast
benumbed space of us, a little more sound to place him.

Were there sour Jewish chives on his tongue,
Yiddish chimes in the bell of his breath?
He knew very little English, but he cocked his ear.

He heard the clock sounds that translate everywhere. He had been brought into redeeming time,
each stroke the echo of his unappearing God.

With tick came the happy interregnum,
those Twenties and Thirties when profit
turned to loss, and loss to profit.

Tock came later when the synagogues swelled
with increase and were tethered like calves
on suburban lawns. And then . . . O and then,

the young walked out, walked back
to the cities, prodigals of emptied memory.
I was among them. And the door slammed shut.

And the space outside, that endlessness to America,
was ululated on every word but tick and tock.

Note to The American Jewish Clock:

Cf. Gen. 17: 4–5: *"As for me, behold, my covenant is with thee, and thou shalt be a father of many nations. Neither shall thy name any more be called Abram, but thy name shall be Abraham; for a father of many nations have I made thee." There are times when I have imagined all the names for things are packed like bricks in a wall, one next to the other, for, in truth, there is no "empty" linguistic space. Not only is all the universe named, but all its openings, voids, and vacuums. The addition to a word of even something as minute as a syllable in a name must therefore, for good or ill, disrupt and displace all the other names that make up reality.*

How, to borrow a phrase from one of George Steiner's essays, has the text become my homeland, my place of most being? My family was American Jewish, playing halfheartedly at religiosity, mainly in accordance with the calendar. That is, we were Jews of the Holy Days, fasting and wearing our solemn faces for the Day of Atonement, anticipating the candles or the feasting of the Passover without much thought of God's injunctions or demands. We sort of sleepwalked through our Jewishness, giving over in the less self-conscious moments of our lives to the mere animal motions, the days and habits of urban city people. Yet thinking about this "going through the motions," which has been characteristic of so many of my generation, I have wondered if this behavior is not a further extension of the text, something we have meant to write with our physical gestures, to "pray," to "sing," to *doven*, like old men, as though we were turning our own personal non-sense, our ritual misunderstandings, self-reflexively into a kind of hunger and longing.

The nonbeliever is aware that, like these religious gestures, talk and writing of a literary-spiritual nature are also performances of degraded rituals. There is no supreme being to hear us talk, and so our silence seems to be achieved finally at the expense of our words, at the exhaustion of our talk. "Silence," as Jabès says, "makes the word audible." But the reverse is also true, that audibility enables us to hear the silence. Such a silence or hushed-ness enshrouding one's life, the resultant of late Jewish catastrophes, gives a sacral meaning to the performative emptiness of the nonbeliever as he acts out the ritual of writing.

How early in my life, I made such an empty sign out of myself, I cannot remember. No matter. For the word *Jewish* was, nevertheless, a forceful word, impelling a direction, an orientation toward the world and history, especially history. History made the Jew a Jew without the person so designated holding any necessary theological principles. The Jew, as Paul Celan poignantly surmised, has "nothing that is not borrowed," least of all the label "Jew." One of the curious mysteries I pondered as a teenager was the crossed nexus of chance and religion. For most people who adhere to a religion, it is not as though one encountered a doctrine and weighed it, but that the religion of one's fathers or nation is perforce a cage or animal trap in which one finds oneself.

To me as a teenager, this trap was essentially the brutal assertion of progenitors. Time and experience alone should have played with me, shaping my moods, my learnings and ultimate desires. But instead, the fathers and grandfathers had reached up from the grave, forced their hands through the crevasses of time and space, to bring the child into their orbit once again. They had commited a crime against Chance itself, had made their religion another weapon of the generational wars, of tradition and custom against spontaneity. Could God have made me a Jew, I asked, before I had the opportunity to do so myself? Such would be my thoughts as I walked to the Temple for some lesson, walked by the playgrounds near my house or peered down the long side streets at the random glitterings of Biscayne Bay.

These inner speculations on being a Jew involved for me the very notion that religion itself is a borrowing, a covering over of one's nakedness, as with Adam and Eve, by the robes of a god. As with a fig leaf, the word or label "Jew" even as it marks out a religious propensity, also sets off the one labelled as still in the world of the profane. The utterance of the word, its distinctiveness, its marking, in essence a *marking off from*, suggests a linguistic equivalent to a dismissal from the Garden.

Such a dismissal seemed a deeply painful "fact" of my early teens when, after the school day ended, I worked in the afternoons for my father, placing promotional leaflets or campaign literature in the lobbies of hotels. It was while doing this work that the word *Jew* became indissolubly linked to the word *Restricted*, a word that appeared in the small type of ads or was conveyed to me by word of mouth about certain hotels that I routinely passed as I walked up Miami Beach's Collins Avenue.

The avenue, the main tourist street of the city, was at that time glamorous and world-famous, with its hundreds of tall white Art Deco hotels neatly trimmed with bands of pale pastel colors. It was also our nighttime playground, a place to drive up and down and talk to young girls in their white dresses spilling out of the brightly lit hotel lobbies like a flood of pale gardenias.

In the heat of the afternoon, however, the avenue, except for the automobile traffic, was usually deserted, the girls and their parents tanning on the beaches or swimming in the pools, places screened off from the public by dense shrubbery and high walls. Then the streets seemed reserved for working people, for waitresses and cleaning women, for men with toolboxes or dressed in waiter and bellhop uniforms scurrying along. I was part of this company, shunted away from the glamor. The heat, as well, was often at its highest, giving the avenue a painful sunblasted air. I dutifully carried my bundles of signs and handouts up that long avenue of brilliant white buildings, often calculating my route by the distance between the shadows cast by the tall buildings, dark rectangles across the pavement and lawns where one might be given a bit of cooling relief. I was even more grateful entering into the vast overly air-conditioned lobbies with their marble floors and tinkling fountains, the sweat under my clothes suddenly going to chill. But I also felt out of place, an intruder in my jeans and dripping T-shirt among the tourists in their blazers and spotless white tennis outfits.

This sense of estrangement was already exacerbated by the semi-impoverishment of my family, impoverishment that made me work while my friends idled away the afternoon at sports or on the beach. It was heightened further whenever I walked by the two "restricted" hotels on my usual route up Collins Avenue. It is hard to believe such places could exist in the mainly Jewish community of Miami Beach, but exist they did. My father had forbidden me to enter these places, but I was both curious and vaguely defiant, and so while I did not go into their lobbies, I often walked up their steps and skirted their patios. I wanted to see what these places were like, who the people were who did not want to associate with me. At one hotel, otherwise normal in all other appearances, there was a discreet "Restricted" sign at the bottom of one of the large plate-glass windows of the entrance. At the other, however, there was no need for a sign, as the building itself was surmounted with a large neon cross which glowed a hideous purple during the day and a pale lavender in the evening.

This latter hotel was a bit rundown. It was squeezed in on a narrow lot between two large and very popular first-class hotels. Its raised patio came nearly to the street. I had a good glimpse of its clientele, who seemed mainly what were called by us "white trash." The men, from my adolescent perspectives of fear and dislike, looked "hard-bitten." They were most likely "crackers" or "rednecks," the appropriate terminology, leathery types, who looked as though they had just been discharged from the army or spent their lives outdoors farming. They were the kind of men I was told by others never to engage in a fight, for these men, with their blue, blood-shot eyes, would sooner die than lose a fight. They would "go for broke," one of my friends said, "unlike us Jews who are reasonable and talk ratio-nalizations and peace."

I am amazed how much the women, the wives or girlfriends of these men, stick in my mind, these women who wore the cheap dresses found in the department stores of small towns. To me, even as I observed them at a distance, they always appeared vaguely depressed, perhaps frightened, almost embarrassed to exist, to be visible. As I measured my pace going by the hotel (I was determined to give no appearance of timidity or fear), I watched these young women who, when smiling or making some pleas-antry, looked anxiously at their men as though they might be overstepping some boundary. And their bodies were as lean and hard as their men's, unlike those of the young women I knew, mostly well-off, who pampered and basted themselves with oils in the sun.

Because of this sense of hardness, I imagined, certain subjects could never be discussed with these people. Whatever conversation, through some strange quirk of circumstances, I might have with these gentiles from the rural South, it must be an evasion, a fearful avoidance of words and conflicts. The handbills I clutched to my chest often carried advertising for some event for the Jewish National Fund or the visit of a famous Yiddish entertainer. They were surely inflammatory materials, inviting ridicule and confrontation from these rednecks or even worse. Thus, in my deliberateness, when I walked by this hotel and glimpsed its clients on the porches and patios, suddenly the long avenue with its waving palm trees and cerulean skies, was a place of guilty silence, the end of language and the possibility of language, of throttling sunlight, of merciless exposure and self-consciousness.

In the world, after the divine interventions at Babel, language is the labelling we do under the sign of a fallen world, for, according to the laws of the first Paradise, which was before Babel, all of Creation moved under the originary names that God allowed Adam to give things. There was nothing to be renamed. But post-Babel . . .

Mankind's linguistic querulousness, the fracturing of the Word into tongues (and, as the Bible would have it, by a jealous God), suggests the theological impossibility of total redemption. Now one perhaps sees or hears God, be it It or She or He, who comes, as it were, from the outside—the very witnessing, the heard tones of Revelation insist on this point—and whose grace or majesty or masked power are then borrowed and made use of. In Judaism, this sense of religion is bound up in the concept of Devekuth, adhesion. One comes face to face with God but does not join Him in mystical union. Every human act, even the most intimately religious, is, therefore, a displacement from God; every prayer, while calling out to God, invoking God, is only testimony to one's apartness from God.

In my teens, when I began to think about the nature of fanaticism, of zealotry, I began to wonder if the distancing from God was not bound up with the intensity of one's religious passion. God fled before the energy of our overactive and acquisitive convictions. Science had not rendered God dead. Rather, His death came from the believer's hand at His throat, by the unspiritual nature of desperate spiritual clinging. In this game, not with God but with ourselves, He had become a horizon, ever receding as we presumed to get closer.

Did that fear of God being apart explain the psychology of my father's careful enunciation of the words of the rituals? That rituals like the Passover seder occurred under a different, separate order of time, outside the flow of quotidian life, did not quite explain my father's recitations, the almost mathematical pursuit of God and ceremony they invoked. All his other talk, I am reminded, did not involve such deliberative tonalities, the tense flexures of his facial muscles, as though reciting a formula. In my father's hopes and in his fears, however vague, words were to deliver him out of his own vagueness and uncertainty. A "religious" life was not the point but that the rituals were occult, ready, and swift conduits to his God.

Words then, sacredness of words, as the words came imperfectly to him. In my late twenties, striving to write poetry, this much of his "religion" seemed vouchsafed to me. Words as applying pressures, as having weight on me rather than referring significantly to things. Words as the very instruments of displacement, propelling one away from them in the way beads of mercury fly from under the hammer. All language was a making of diasporas and scatterings. In my thoughts, in my immature yet Ur-poetic sensibility, words were not free standing. I could not wander through a landscape of representations, thinking and choosing "tree," "house," "bread," "lover." I was instead to take them up as vectors, snarled in complications, and having unwanted and unasked for meanings and representations attached. In this sense, language resembled the house of my father, not as a Law but as a series of illusions and difficulties, a structure of facades like my father's face. When he felt required to mask his disappointments or to play the jolly fellow for his friends, when I "read" him thus, it was simply the operations of the Janus-faced law of the Word. In truth, I associate his dissembling with the world of Letters, with its extraordinary displacements and misreadings, its elusive and belated processing of information, its profound and tragic doubledness.

Thus, even when I first began to write, I felt compelled to negotiate the drifts and currents of words as a sailing craft would maneuver in troubled waters in a high wind. It was not that words did not or could not represent precisely, but that always on the other side was this entanglement, this "otherness" to a word's usage, this meaning which you had never meant for the word but which someone might yet take up, thwarting your purposes and hopes. Jacques Derrida, in his reflections on Celan's poetry, identifies the poet's use of a word with the act of circumcision, to cut off and to circumscribe, to free the word from historical entrapment. If one's purposes were bound up in something we might call "poetic," one's meaning would have to be divided off from all others. Therefore, the violence of usage was not all on one side. Poetry writ large could only be experienced as a death knell, a sounding against one from the other side of words.

In a sense, then, to write poetry meant to write amidst ruins, to pipe on the reed of life in a charnel ground. In the unavoidable overhearings of a word, in its associative dimensions—Walter Benjamin referred to this as the word's aura—there resided something sinister, the awful fullness of history, the other "ruins" which language could not only describe but had aided in creating: what humanity had made of the world. Thus, words, even as they participated in the realm of nostalgia and evoked golden ages, even as they brought glories and prides before the imagination, inscribed lostness. For Jewish practice, which consists of placing layer upon layer of borrowings and accretions, lostness made something cosmic out of dispersal and diaspora.

IN A DARK TIME, ON HIS GRANDFATHER

Zalman Heller, writer and teacher, d. 1956

There's little sense of your life
Left now. In Cracow and Bialystok, no carcass
To rise, to become a golem. In the ground

The matted hair of the dead is a mockery
Of the living root. Everyone who faces
Jerusalem is turned back, turned back.

It was not a question of happiness
Nor that the Laws failed, only
That the holy or sad remains within.

This which cleft you in the possibility
Of seeing Him, an old man
Like yourself.

Your last years, wandering
Bewildered in the streets, fouling
Your pants, a name tag in your coat

By which they led you back,
Kept leading you back. My father
Never spoke of your death,

The seed of his death, as his death
To come became the seed, etc. . . . Grandfather,
What to say to you who cannot hear?

The just man and the righteous way
Wither in the ground. No issue,
No issue answers back this earth.

Note to In A Dark Time, On His Grandfather:

"The just man and the righteous way." A rumor circulated in my family that my grand-father, who, in addition to his rabbinical work, had written poetry, essays, and children's fiction, was the author of a Talmudic study entitled The Just Man And The Right-eous Way. *No extant copy of this work has ever been found.*

Before literature or poetry, there were rockets on the golf course. I was twelve years old, and from discarded CO_2 cartridges, the shiny steel ones used at home for making soda water, I fashioned miniature projectiles, soldering onto the tails little metal fins cut from old coffee or tuna fish cans. Then I packed them with powder shaken out of firecrackers or mixed my own with drugstore saltpeter and sulfur. Launched into the air from the grassy fairways of the unused and deserted old municipal golf course on Miami Beach's Pinetree Drive not far from my home, they arced into the sky on a plume of black smoke with a nearly inaudible whistling. If there was heavy traffic on Pinetree Drive, it was as though my little missiles were sailing on silence toward the clouds.

At that time, I was the youngest member of the American Rocket Society and read with a feverish interest the articles in the newsletter and the books in the public library by Robert Goddard, Wernher von Braun, and Willy Ley. Rocketry was still scoffed at by the military-industrial establishment, and the articles of the Journal of the Society, a crudely published broadside with fuzzy pictures, like an anti-establishment literary magazine, portrayed the rocket-making community as a group of embattled pioneers and prophets. Photos of Goddard showed him standing beside primitive Rube Goldberg–like contraptions of metal tubing and struts, all of it held together with baling wire.

But the Second World War had transformed reality and nearly erased America's pastoral quality for good. And here, Goddard and Ley were its Futurists and Lettrists, members of a new avant-garde who would inscribe a sky neither with the sun-brilliant blues of the Hudson River School nor with the Magritte bowlers of the surrealists, but with a spectral geometry of trajectories, orbits, and interception points. For the catastrophes that fell across the world—and the Cold War that followed them—had, as well, brought into being a new language, a language infused not by the vocabularies of books or the humanistic sciences but by the plotted torques of carbon steel, by crystallography and telemetered circuits.

I suppose that, as a young person, I was hearing something strange, powerful, and beyond evaluation in these new wordings and formulations, something alternately thrilling and frightening. The Hebrew passages which I was memorizing for my Bar Mitzvah, even as they reminded one of God's severe power and judgment, struck me as anachronistic and distant compared to these new verbal technologies, these compactions that actually named, defined, and captured the world around me.

Later, after I had finished engineering school, but still before poetry, in that period in my life when I was totally awash in a miasma of post-college drinking, cars, girlfriends, parties, my self-aware thought found limited corollaries in science and engineering.

I had graduated with a scientific degree from school and was earning a living from technical writing. Yet it was not that I was particularly good at working in any area involved with these things; rather, they appealed to my young man's search for certain exactitudes, for some sense in which the mind seemed to touch the real world at points. Spengler's *Decline of the West*, which I read in my twenties, with its injunctions against metaphysics and humanistic romanticisms, was a doctrine, however benighted, of spiritual *realpolitik*. Technology was the spirit of the times, and its encodings, its rules, its methodological efficiencies and demonstrations were quite possibly the rubrics and homilies one ought to live by. Furthermore, the practice of science had a ritualistic, disinterested flavor: what, after all, was holier than a laboratory and its calibrated instruments or the arcane, priestly language of scientific discipline.

In the deepest sense, the scientific search *was* religious. It had as its *raison d'être*, the world's existence. Science, from the point of view of language, even at its most abstracted, still held the dream of perfect representation. It could purify language, miraculously converting observation into syntax and linguistics, and so free language of the unneeded dross of misunderstanding. Science, so understood, was angelic metaphor, metaphor which spoke accurately of the Creation surrounding God's throne. To give weight and measure was an activity which, although it did not complete knowledge, at least secured a certain kind of silence, momentarily freed of existential doubt.

This silence was prayerful, an invocation or confirmation: the mind of man and that of the Creator had momentarily meshed. This was the message of the seventeenth-century poets and writers such as Browne and Vaughan who versed earthly gardens and Harmoniums of multiple orderings. It was their poems, above all others, that performed closures the way one shuts tight a ritual book, a hymnal or prayer-reader.

I could understand that for such poets, the Messiah, in Jesus, had come. For me, the Jewish poet's not-at-homeness reflected the absence of Messianic fulfillment. In the works of the Jewish writer like Agnon or Kafka, one heard a kind of keening, a bewailing of distance from the Temple. Even the Jewish poem of praise, of beauty seen and taken in, argued and hectored over the incompleteness of God's world. Such poetry could only find its true moment as dread or prophecy.

Poetry, at least in my young mind, embodied two vast and contradictory human tropes: the urge toward meaning, with no residue left, i.e., with the sufficiency of a scientific discourse; and the urge to reveal a world beyond present limitations, not merely as some Romantic poet's figuring, some "inner dictation," but as a method by which one moved beyond boundaries, beyond conceptual schemes.

This still left unanswered the moment of silence, the closure of poem or ritual when one was thrown back into the profane world. What I now think of as Jewish silence, which emulates that silence of science, the other side of precision, so to speak, struck me, when later I had decided to write poetry, as a fearful place to enter, a "no-space," dimensionless and unmapped. For the pious Jew, this silence possibly suggested gaps in creation, the great crack in Revelation. In this essentially kabbalistic view, silence would be how God filled up the awesome flaw in the universe and forced wonder and majesty, and even contrition, upon man.

And yet humankind, it struck me, was unable to hold its tongue in its response to wonder, and so filled up silence with a kind of noise. Poetry, literature, a religious tradition such as the Judaic one of endless commentary, these all might constitute an anxiety-ridden logorrhea meant to plaster over with spilled words the perceived lacunae of existence.

My own awareness, part anxiousness and part love of language, though never self-enunciated, was perhaps as much Buddhistic as Jewish, a sense of the simultaneous apprehension of emptiness and fullness, that endless arena in which things hover on existence and nonexistence simultaneously. Such a possibility of reality seemed confirmed in the polysemy of midrashic literature, which accepts all understandings of the world as partial fulfillments of divine understanding. I felt—in fact desperately needed to feel— that the word or poem marginally edged the real, that it limned a figure of the mind—but of whose mind? This was the basic question, one that was concerned with divinity or, more accurately, the possibility of divinity. The poem was not meant to depict or replicate certain realities of a political or moral nature, nor was it meant to illustrate the difficulties of poetic construction (this the most prevalent ongoing trap). Rather, the poem was a series of steps, a method of relief, a wandering in the desert after mirage or actual water. It meant little which of these was to be found.

Had my parents discussed their pasts with me, perhaps many matters would now be cleared up. Or so one would like to believe, an idea, I think, that accounts now for those violent appeals to one's race, origin, nationality. In a world more uncertain than ever, personal and racial memories are gathered, hoarded against the vast seas of anxiety and doubt that are eroding the boundaries of the self. And yet, now, every word or memory used to make one more substantial may only be a crime against one's own self-freedom—and carried to extremes, such a word must inevitably become drenched in blood.

What I am "doing" here, marshalling remembrances, I sense, is not history but something closer to science or poetry. In fact, as one accumulates the past as an exercise in memory, all kinds of curious and even unpleasant facts build up, enclosing one in the claustrophobias of historical time. *Did I get this gesture from my mother or my father? Where has this face led me, what people has it attracted or rejected? What do I honestly love or hate?* The fileboxes of memory, each with a motive attached, spill over, and each marked sheet of the past is lifted from the floor of Time as though one were examining a riddle. Then the question becomes not only what but how do you remember? At last, you have understood that each mote of time is not a memory stamp for your collection but a piece of original research, a fact one must walk around and finally place in the landscape of a new day.

So, in a sense, I may very well have been aided by my parents' reticence. For like many first-generation or youthful newcomers, they were looking ahead rather than behind. The past that seems to be restored by my acts of reflection (a typical second-generation activity) was what they were trying to distance themselves from. There was very little family reminiscing, only unfilled gaps. Even the colorful Yiddish on which they had been nourished was used, in our household, as a means of secretive communication, of discussing things we children were not supposed to hear. The gap then was also linguistic or at least made so by the dissonance between the two modes of speech.

It was such gaps that possibly led my uncle Nat a few years ago, in a comic moment of biographical endeavor, to obtain, from some genealogical service, the Heller coat of arms—on the basis of which I am actually a Scotsman!

How then to approach the past? Merleau-Ponty, the French philosopher writes: "Two things are certain about freedom; that we are never determined and yet that we never change, since looking back on who we were, we can always find hints of what we have become. It is up to us to understand both things simultaneously." To this I would add: I reflect back, but the past which is my object does not contain my thought of the past. When I remember back, when I try to perceive *back*, I revise and disfigure the very chronologies I am mounted upon. These chronologies, accruing moment by moment, are like a rising mountain peak, something being constructed under me, or—to reshape a figure borrowed from Walter Benjamin—historical time, in all its grand and minute plenitudes, constitutes the thrust, the long cone of flaring gases of a rocket, and I am that rocket's payload into the future. But when I reflect back, when I interrupt by slicing a cross-section, some stopped image of *my time* (no one else's), I break with that deterministic flow, the impelling of me toward unreflected fate.

Such reflection has it risks, for the image has two powers: one to fix a moment, and that can in itself become overwhelming and determinative, a power I would associate with nostalgia or guilt (this I did, for this I must always suffer). But the other power of the image, to break the unreflected processes that propel one along, the unknown borrowings and habitual patterns—to rupture these, is to awaken one's self from a living sleep.

When I enter across time with reflection on a little story or incident, my thought shatters time's unidirectional power the way sailors threw their harpoons and other objects into the swirling trunks of waterspouts to diffuse and disperse their force. In this sense, the act of autobiography, the making of a memoir is not the creation of literary form, one that putatively says, here is Michael Heller's life. True, Michael Heller is here and remains. Nothing can dissolve the fact that *I* gaze, that *I* reflect and reorder, but here *I* is not so much a thing as an act and a task. Because for time to come, one is free. As Rousseau writes in the *Confessions*: "[W]e never do anything but begin. . . . [O]ur existence is nothing more than a series of present moments." Memoir then can be a way of derailing or re-ordering a life, a way of re-seeing the world, not as the cumulations of history, but as the arena of possibility.

FOR UNCLE NAT

I'm walking down 20th Street with a friend
When a man beckons to me from the doorway
Of Congregation Zichron Moshe. "May I,"
He says to my companion, "borrow this
Jewish gentleman for a moment?" I follow
The man inside, down the carpeted aisle,
Where at the front, resplendent in
Polished wood and gold, stands
The as yet unopened Ark.

Now the doors slide back, an unfolded
Promissory note, and for a moment,
I stand as one among the necessary ten.
The braided cloth, the silver mounted
On the scrolls, even the green of the palm
Fronds placed about the room, such hope
Which breaks against my unbeliever's life.

So I ask, Nat, may I borrow you, for a moment,
To make a necessary two? Last time we lunched,
Enclaved in a deli, in the dim light, I saw
A bit of my father's face in yours. Not to make
Too much of it, but I know history
Stamps and restamps the Jew; our ways
Are rife with only momentary deliverance.
May I borrow you for a moment, Nat. We'll celebrate
By twos, the world's an Ark. We'll talk in slant,
American accent to code the hidden language of the Word.

Note to For Uncle Nat:

Cf. Gen. 11: 6–8: *God speaks: "Behold, the people is one, and they have one language; and this they begin to do: and now nothing will be restrained from them, which they have imagined to do. Go to, let us go down, and there confound their language, that they may not understand one another's speech." The second expulsion from Paradise was at Babel. When the tower was built to reach unto heaven, and a unifying name was to be fashioned from the common language which all mankind spoke, the angels were sent to scatter men lest they rival God in their doings. And yet, if the unity of language was broken at Babel, in every separate tongue, in every participle and phrase of a language, the old unity must be hinted at. Each piece of a language, a word, a letter, a sentence, can be likened to a sliver of porcelain from which a shattered cup can be envisioned and reconstructed. Indeed, it could also be demonstrated that the scattering that was Babel was also the entrance into a new Paradise of the richness of many tongues. A multiplicity of languages (and even the sublanguages, argots, slangs, and dialects within a language) make all utterances into dialogues, for it is only through the recognition of differences—or even misunderstandings—that full communication can begin. This multiplicity of languages would constitute a number of theophanies, traceries of the divine logos which thread through individuals, family groups, cultures, and nations and so animate the biblical story. Martin Buber remarks in* I and Thou *that primary words do not signify things but intimate relationships. He concludes that the religious sphere lies "between beings." The modern world, then, in which contact with many cultures is a global phenomenon, would not be so much a case of "After Babel" as a working back toward Babel by yet another means. The hope of unity, of meaning for each other as well as for ourselves, would be the haunting that all speaking and writing enacts, the "hidden language" that is summonable in each linguistic act.*

Cf. Emily Dickinson, No. 1129: "Tell all the truth but tell it slant—"

My grandfather became the model of the distant God, faintly irrelevant. . . . It was his way of speaking, the flat hum of syllables . . . the *dovening* in synagogue. Against this was the equally ancient principle of copying out, the practice of Walter Benjamin, a route to the physical, material substance of words, also a way to register their exactitude. The Kabbalists seemed to have feared, more than anything else, misreading or miscopying. This latter way was my father's, his recitations from the *Haggadah* had about them the anxious hoverings of a man tiptoeing along the top rail of a fence, the way of fear.

The brackish Atlantic, intermingled with the other oceans of the world, and which separated the Hellers of Bialystok from the Hellers of Brooklyn, also came, like the physical embodiment of some unwritten dynamic, to separate my father from his father. Within only a few years of the family's arrival in America, some combination of my grandfather's sternness and a son's youthful wanderlust drove my father from the house. As I have reconstructed my grandfather's image from both photographs and memories, and the few reminiscences of my aunts and uncle, the purported rigor and sternness of his character strikes me less as a fact than as a type of invention of my father's, not unlike my own creation of my greatgrandfather. Even as I write of my own parents, I am thinking that the one law of family life is not that children are like their parents but that they must, in order to grow, misinvent, misread, and misunderstand them. This is the truth of the fact that the grandfather on whose lap I played and who pinched my cheeks and tickled my ribs, also, in his very being, marched my father to the doors of the world.

On U.S.S. Turrialba

1918

MY FATHER, a runaway at age sixteen, a cook's mate, leaning against the rail. "Sorry I left but too late to return now."

Only fifteen, my father somehow managed to secure a job as a cook's mate on the *SS Turrialba*, a ship owned by the United Fruit Lines that plied the Atlantic between South America, Europe, and New York. He had been aided in his escape, I don't know how, by his brother Nat, a few years older and envious that he was not escaping too. A letter from my father sent to Nat hints at the confining family atmosphere from which he had sought escape. It also shows my father, aged fifteen, with a flair for the literary, for a certain dramatic edge to his language:

Antwerp, Belgium   October 17. 1919

Dear Nathan,

I am sorry I had to leave home but the talk talk and talk about the bums drove me from home. I am sorry I left but it is too late to return now. I have a very nice gold plated wirebelt for you and a knife a foot long which was given to me by an officer for my good service. If you don't mind send me my overcoat and some old pants, yours are torn now. I sew, iron and wash my old clothes. Tell mama I made a mistake. I get $150 . . . for two months besides eats and clothes. Here is a little incident on the boat which almost made me return home. It was Sunday October 12, 1919. The night was calm, and the moon and stars were shining and a nice cool breeze was blowing. The passengers were seated on the deck smoking and laughing and singing old songs. Suddenly one of them proposed to two young boys to play some song that will remind them of home. They consented and one took out a violin and one sang. They sang a few songs and I became interested and I sat on a wire ladder and listened and as I listened they sang "O Dear Old Pal of Mine" and as they sang this sad song the sweet voices of the boy and the violin reminded me of an angel standing alone begging God to take him back and when I thought of this memories

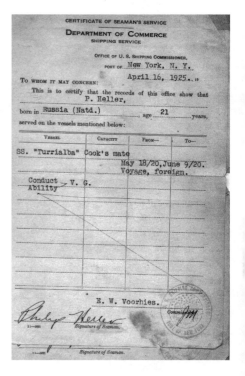

MY FATHER'S working papers.

dear to me came back. Memories of life at home, of school and friends. I was wondering to myself, why I gave up home, reputation and friendship and everything that was dear to me. Why I left home like a crook in the dark night like one forsaken and hated by everyone. Why I left my pal my mother to seek new lands. When I thought of that I cried and wanted to return home. But I took out the Bible and read a psalm to David saying Hope again and etc. and when I finished my courage came back to me and told me to go be a man and show the mettle you are made from and I did.

When you read this and imagine this you will cry too. And for God's sake don't leave home like I did. Home is the shining light that brings you to success. My light will be my memory of home.

Your brother Philip Heller

P.S. Please send out *tphilim* and other things and pictures of home. I'll send $100.00 home through my agent.

P.S. I have German, Belgium and French money for you.
Don't worry.
Please send a *haftorah* and English, Jewish papers
Give my regards to Jennie, Ina and Bessie.

Many times, I have reread this letter, which my uncle Nat showed to me only after my father had died, finding myself in envious thrall to its youthful melo-drama. A ghostly power resides in its words. For thinking back on my father's ruination in his illness, remembering that bright gleam of jealousy which flashed from his eyes on that day long ago when I pronounced to him my intentions to be a writer, I have a distinct feeling that this letter of his con-stitutes a kind of revenge, speaking beyond the grave against my pretentions, against all those little self-satisfied flarings of what we call literary.

After a passage from Europe to South America, my father wrote to Nat again:

United Fruit Company
Steamship Service
On Board

Mr Nat Heller

Arrived in Puerto Columbia Columbia S. A. I will send some souvenirs and money from there.

Dear Nat, I finished the letter already but I want to tell you one thing how sorry I was when I left you on the dock after you sacrificing every-thing for me. I swore I don't go on the next boat till you go with me. You don't know how I was crying when I saw your shape moving further away from your brother. I tell you Nathan I am sorry I went without you.

Phil

After poring over much of the material I have accumulated concerning my father's life, these two shipboard letters mark for me the only moments of pure graspability, the only time I feel I have a sense of my father in my hand. Possibly that speaks as much for me as for my sense of my father, for I deeply admire his courage here, his language, his sentimental idealism of family. This image I have of him radiates back at me, investing me with its qualities. It is as though, for a moment, the code of my being were born not in the parental gene but in the syntax and vocabulary of his utterance, of the letter's verbal ideality. It would be true to say, to confess, that all my fathers and mothers have so come to me on the carrier bands of language.

Of my father, the grammatical particle of myself, the partitive, that which I have shared, that which I have moved from. Biology is destiny but so is language. I am trying to construct him here, not reconstruct, because I am now speaking of periods before my birth, and the father I know (or knew) while growing up is someone quite different from the youthful distillates of these two letters.

Kierkegaard, in *Fear and Trembling*, stages the drama of Abraham and Isaac, of father and son, across the tangential surfaces of imagination and thinking. Abraham, leading Isaac to Mount Moriah, the place of sacrifice, heavy-hearted with the duty required of him, is focused not on the rewards of faith but on the "shudder of thought," the conceptual impossibility that he must murder his own son. In writing here, as a son, I must too take up the matter of sacrifice, for I too have become what I have become not only because of my father's strengths but on the altar of his weaknesses. That is, I visualize these failings of his as porosities, flaws and openings through which a son might flee a father or in which, through proud rebellion, a son might grow as weeds through the seams of paving stones. The altar then, the sacrifical shrine stone, is mazed with cracks through which the fluidities of spirit, the self (the totalizing term is lost to our usage) would flow, reconstituting itself into a new wholeness. My escape into whatever "myself" has become is *out from under*.

I deliver this escape, I affirm it, as counter-blow, counter-memory in the act of rewording the father in the text, in replaying or transgressing Freud by insisting that in this work the father is child to the man. For me, such transgression works something like this: in memory, in historical device and artifact, *I* am the Abraham who ponders the sacrifice of the Isaac who is image, the youthful but now repositioned father image which

I constructed as a child out of idealistic desire and hidden fears and which now I have brought, as though it were a tribute, to the altarstone of later knowledge and understanding.

Now too, I believe, my love for him is more complete for in writing about him from this late perspective I have found the place of its wording, as Kierkegaard did, in the place between "the ingenious web of imagination" and the belated shudder.

One reverts to letters, to photographs, to an archeology of chance *documenta*. One lays these diffidently on the cold stones of the altar. What is lost is lost, but even more, there is nothing to be found. The biographical and the autobiographical processes are, in some sense, allegorical but are blindsided to the full, if fictive, idea of a continuous life. Out of the residue of history and memory a few items are thrown up and the chronicler who connects these dots, so to speak, does so only as a fictional practice. Rather, the construction of an individual biographically is like Zeno's paradox of the arrow in flight which can never get to its destination because it must incrementally halve the remaining distances no matter how minute. The gaps in memory or in those expanses of black mounting paper that lie between the items in a scrapbook; these, too, are half-sundered increments. One is bound to miss certain significant moments, shifts of being or consciousness. History making, personal or otherwise is a matter not of filling out a portrait but of seeing a life as a version of quantum mechanics.

The invented purity of my father, by which I mean a certain truth-function (for me and me alone) in those letters from the *SS Turrialba* are at odds with the tonal emanations of later material fished out of the Heller tidal pools of time. And the dissonances between these documents, rather than the singularity of any specific event, are what make me perceive him as a tragic figure. Tragic figures require their tragic flaws and, as I have suggested already, my father's flaw was his peculiar sentimental streak, a feeling about the world that was too weak to sustain his idealism and yet, powerful enough to play monkey business with his desires to be and to seem to be a man of substance and affairs. Any "life" so examined, I suspect, would reveal much the same dissonances; any life can be written as tragic, not because of the difference between the letter and the deed but because of that between image and image, word and word, and, in my father's case, literally between letter and letter.

If, as Wittgenstein tells us, each utterance presents a picture of reality, then a man or a woman is drawn by words, most assuredly by the world their utterance predicates. But what then of the discontinuities of which we each seem constructed? What are the allotropes of personality that discover us at one time in state A and at another in state B? Surely the lacunae between these states are an area of contemplation.

One marker of dissonant transformation in my father's case may simply be a bit of occult if minor onomastics. At some point in my father's early twenties, he began signing letters and referring to himself not only by his given name Philip but also by the name Peter (usually shortened to Pete except for the most formal situations, business signatures, letterheads). For awhile the two names were both used: Philip, as far as I can tell from the documentation I have, seeming to represent the idealistic son of Zalman Heller who ran away to sea. Peter, or more often Pete is the signature of a slightly corrupted and corrupting person, one whose ideals simultaneously turned treacly and self-deceptive.

For example: On February 19th, 1926, my father (now signing his mail "Pete" rather than Phil or Philip) writes to his sister Ida (later called Ina) at the family residence at 329 Quincy Street, Brooklyn, N.Y. The return address on the envelope, Florida Productions, Inc, Motion Pictures, 1508 Grand Central Avenue, Tampa, Florida, is that of one of my father's failed businesses, a movie production company that would employ as actors the famous baseball players, such as Dazzy Vance, Dizzy Dean, John J. McGraw, and Ty Cobb, who would be in the Tampa area for spring training. My father writes:

Dear Ida,

Perhaps you will be a little surprised to hear from me again, nevertheless, I find it very necessary to write to you so that you may communicate with some member of the family to comply with my wish. . . .

I remember I asked you to forward me telephone books including the New York City Red Book which you haven't done as yet. I wish you would take care of that as soon as possible as that is an item which I most assuredly need in my business and in my new ventures in Tampa. Enough of that.

Now this matter which I am going to mention to you in the following paragraph is very important and I want you to follow directions strictly to the letter. If I am not mistaken you are still employed by the same firm that you have been working for when I left home. I also remember that your employer handles a line of novelties. I will very much appreciate if you could communicate with him and tell him that I would be very glad to handle his various lines on some basis that we can arrange.

There is a great field for anything new in Florida. And as I know the state very well and the means of approaching trade here I am sure we could do business together in a way beneficial to us both. Dear Sis—put this up to him as strong as you can because I can put it across. If necessary give me his address and let him communicate with me. Also write me in the meantime and tell me what success I can look forward to.

Your brother Pete is hustling for business now and is full of pep. If you handle your end right I am confident I can give him satisfaction and business he desires in this territory.

This is all for today and I want you to do your best along the lines I have sketched above and we will get along quite nicely. With best regards to Father and Mother,

Your brother,

Pete

My father's slippage from idealistic runaway into the sometime less than effectual con man of this letter to Ida/Ina poses enormous questions for the son, who, attempting to grasp his own temporality, looks at every dot, every emerged mark of a life, not only as a fact but as a cause and an effect. "My courage," my father, aged fifteen, wrote to Nat, but speaking of an interior monologue to himself, "told me to go be a man and show the mettle you are made from." But if there was any courage to be found in the letter to Ina, it was only that of desperation, of nervous audacity, with a ring so hollow that the word "hustling" is a bit of an abrasion on this later reader's heart.

To write at these junctures where recollections meet is to be making up a language, more specifically to be making up a word or a name (in the larger poetic sense of naming) by conjoining two disparate terms. In the strata of memory which I tap here, my father's name is suddenly Philip Peter, an oxymoron.

One speculative flight I take up is that Philip is my father's legal name and in that name he does things legally. Peter (etymologically derived from *petrus*, stone) is a harder character, translatable in my father's use of it as willed ignorance or guileful bluntness, as less sensitive to certain nuances and niceties. Two and half years after the letter to Ina, Pete is again Philip, embossed in gold on the announcement of his wedding to my mother. Other than for extremely official purposes, that is Philip's last appearance: the Pete of my father now covers over the Rabbi's son's soul. Not totally, for soulful Philip swims up out of the depths in the family arena to love his children, to love and succor his ailing wife.

I detect also—again, the evidence is fragmentary—that a physiognomic change occurs with the trading away of names. Absurdly, from earliest infancy through mid-twenties, every photograph of my father as a Philip looks as though its fixing bath were the liquor of idealized romance and virtue; the face of Philip longs, searches as though beyond this world, is deep and gentle, a mother's angel. Philip Heller is photographed a year or two after returning from his merchant marine service wearing khakis in a forest clearing, leaning on the handle of an axe, a felled tree under his right foot. Beneath the photograph is a little squib of a story, my father's byline, extolling the wonders of the open air, the comraderie of hard work and clean living. Another photograph shows Philip in a black, tank-type swimsuit. He is sitting on a boulder by the edge of a lake, deep in contemplation. Tall pines surround this slim, handsome thinker as he gazes off into the unspoiled depths of Nature.

Not much later, "Pete" (now replacing "Philip") appears, so the caption reads, in a photograph. In place of the idealistic romantic youth, we have pictured a laughing ironic fellow standing in front of the offices of the motion picture company with a cigar in his mouth. Pete smiles too much. Captured in the silvered emulsion there is also an undercurrent of romance, but it is that of the movie idol; charm, but also the cleverness that knows it ought to please. In another photograph, he is surrounded by his baseball player-actors, John McGraw and Dizzy Dean, I am told, under the waving palms of Tampa. A motion picture camera on a tripod stands to one side. "Pete" will wear this same hat when he moves on to sell lots for his real estate firm, Rubber City Plantations, playing the banjo, huckstering the gathered folk near some mosquito-infested swamp.

It is not that Philip and Pete look so different that they seem like two different people, rather it is like looking at the masks of Janus, two

PHILIP ("Pete") Heller
in the woods, 1925.

hammered gold
charms hung from
adjacent beads on
the memory chains.
How to get from
one face to the next?

Indeed, despite
my father's promises
and hopes, the
motion picture
company shortly
went bust, and my
father moved on
into that other
bubble of opti-
mism, Florida's late-
Twenties real estate boom. The Brooklyn boys who had helped form the
motion picture company and now jumped into the Florida real estate game,
all of them Jewish and all from the neighborhood, were occasionally home-
sick, I am told. They were not religious, but raised for so many years on the
kosher diets of their parents, they were physically repelled by Southern
cooking with its pork and lard. They had salamis mailed to them from up
North, and bought canned tuna fish by the case. They dressed "nattily,"
which would be the word, adorned in three-piece suits and straw boaters in
nearly all the photographs I have of this period. The hair is slicked back, the
style of the day, but also invoking a semiotics of charm and minor villainy.

The real estate "venture" (I want now to put that word in my father's
voice) was something of a sham. The operating equipment of the firm consisted of a mule-drawn wagon on which was mounted a large subdivision

map, showing lots and acreage. The Brooklyn boys, donning their boaters and taking off their dark jackets in the heat, had brought musical instruments along and strummed up tunes to raise a crowd. My father played the banjo. When a decent-sized group of people was assembled, the lots were described and bids taken. The customers were mostly the poor whites of Tampa, perhaps with a few greedy speculators tossed in. Many years later, my father confessed to me that some of the land was nothing more than swamp.

Throughout these occasions and on up until his death, what remains a permanent feature of my father's character is his romanticism and sentimentality, a vulnerability that saved him from the worst excesses of chicanery. Needless to say, it kept him fairly broke as well.

My father's two names had almost no sound in common save the plosiveness of the final "p" of Philip and the "P" of Pete (or Peter). Spinning out some kabbalistic game of linguistic signs, I might conjure that it is by

PETE ("Philip") Heller in front of Florida Productions, Inc., Motion Pictures, Tampa, Florida, 1926.

MY FATHER'S photograph of the pitcher Dazzy Vance, one of his "movie stars."

those common "p" sounds that the names are linked across one individual life. But also, that the remaining differences in sound between the two names might signal complex, even contradictory, psychic divergences. Sound and orthography as matters of fate?

I am reminded that many commentators on the Torah regard Revelation as something that is heard. The intimations of Paradise, of a Messiah come, are first (and perhaps last) auditory phenomena. Yet if hearing is the gate of Revelation, then what is to be heard must set itself off from the ongoing noise of human life, from the background of our doings and traffickings. In Genesis, Abram, when he is to be the recipient of God's Promised Land, is thereafter named Abraham by God. This new name, setting off the one renamed, because it signifies difference, is a constant reminder of the redeemed nature of Abraham and his people, of the holy pact he has been enjoined to enter.

Such onomastic activity, like the renaming that occurs in initiation rites or in joining religious orders, is often central to the Scriptural message. It signals a radical change or transformation in the life of the individual who is renamed. The most well-known, and most puzzled-over renaming concerns the story of Jacob's wrestling with the Angel (or, as Harold Bloom and others have intimated, with the Angel of Death). Jacob is victorious, and receives the special blessing that lies at the heart of Jewish culture: he is henceforth given the name of Israel (meaning "may God persevere"). Newness, such as that celebrated by renaming, even as it is purposeful, is reflexive of the creative powers inherent in the universe.

The memory of the old names? What you were, what you need no longer be? A new name is a kind of effacement, the making of one's self into a new clean slate upon which to inscribe one's own or God's work. In effect, a discrete, inspiriting piece of language. And yet, all names are born and have meaning only *between* the erasure of the old and the inscription of the new. The possibility of transcendence, from error into light (or the reverse), depends upon the contrast. For no memory has been erased: a new name, even the most sacred, is not a lobotomy.

To take up Derrida's metaphor again, renaming, as the prototypical activity of the poet, heals the circumcision-like wound of existence, the covenantal mark. Momentarily, the word covers the breach, the poet's psychic chasm, but its work is immediately undone as the poem passes into the province of interpreters and critics (among these, of course, the author of the poem).

As any anthropologist will testify, all cultures re-name. Surely it was so in the mini-culture of the Hellers. In fact, the signet of my own and my family's history constitutes, not only births and deaths, but at times a kind of onomancy or re-onomancy. When I think of renamings, these little asides come to mind:

— When Henry Smith discarded his Eastern European name, he was hoping to discard as well its metonymies of ghetto and *shtetl* life. Not a particularly noble act, perhaps. But that he took the name "Smith," the most common of names, one totally uncharacteristic of his ways of being or his appearance, strikes me as another instance of his ironic turn of mind. I sense, on his part, a deep reluctance to abolish or mute his status. Rather, given his unmistakeable "Jewishness," such a name establishes "Smith" as the purest of aliases, drawing the hearer of such a name who is standing before "Smith," the person, into the complicity, the need, for the name change itself. What an elegant solution, enabling the name to be worn honorably, while at the same time suggesting that it is "society" that forced this change upon its bearer, even as it was "society" in Europe that forced the yellow star upon the Jew.

— Zalman to Solomon Heller. My grandfather had come to America and experienced the transliteration of his first name. A clerk at the Ellis Island Immigration desk undoubtedly rewrote it. All the stories of name changes by such clerks, with all their pathos and hilarity, still strike a deeper, almost Kafkaesque note, of whole families and generations suddenly and arbitrarily being verbally uprooted. The ultimate purpose of a bureaucracy operating on its own internal rules and codes may be to ignore circumstance, history, individuality and assign names as though they were numbers, to normalize its world. This official normalization seemed to have the effect of sealing my grandfather in a tin can or mason jar where his Eastern European habits were preserved like plums in syrup. The biblical Solomon saved the to-be-divided child; the Heller Solomon, himself undivided, nevertheless, stood at the head of a new lineage of divided children, my father and his brothers and sisters, me and mine. For us, the "old country" was a myth to be inhabited only by looking at a picture book or to be used as a stopper when reality was running out of a sinkhole in the present. And yet, I must account my grandfather's emigration a true myth, for it explains my existence. Without that step across the Atlantic, the Holocaust would have written *finis* to the possibility of there even being a *me*.

— And so I contemplate again my father who was born Philip, who ran away from home at the age of fifteen and went to sea, never to truly reside again with his father. His formative years, when his personality was being shaped, were spent on boats, at odd jobs, away from his father's influence. Somewhere, he began to call himself and came to be called Peter, the first name by which I knew him for most of my life.

But what about the morphology of how we are called which pursues us throughout our lives? It too is a series of sounds, though it is that of a rushing cascade impelling us toward our futures: In 1943, Peter ("Pete" to his close pals) F. Heller, Captain, 13th Regiment, New York State National Guard, commission signed by one of his Republican clubhouse cronies in Albany, will be photographed leading a march up Pulaski Street,

Brooklyn, right past No. 172, our house, where my mother, Martha, my sister, Tena (born "Ernestine"), my older brother, Bummy (his birthname was "Avrom"), and I will be sitting on the high brownstone stoop looking down at the parade and cheering. Captain Heller will be wearing an Army issue Colt .45 in the holster on his right side supported by a handsome thin leather strap slung sideways from his left shoulder across his chest. His moustache is neatly trimmed, and he is still tall and elegant but with a slight middle-aged paunch which the belt cuts into. President of the Dade County Democratic Club, Peter F. Heller of Peter F. Heller Associates, 100 Lincoln Road, Miami Beach, Florida, greets Lyndon Baines Johnson at the Miami City Hall where the president will receive the Key to the City.

Ah Philip, Peter, Pete, Pa, Dad, whoever, wearing a baseball cap tilted comically off your head as you sit in a wheelchair in the Miami Beach Nursing Home where all the black nurses who wash your urine-stained underwear pinch your cheek and call you "Pops!"

III

I AM THREADING the beads of an amulet; the string is made of intuition. The father bead and the mother bead are proximate, and held not by string but by a clasp. The substance of that clasp, linking the entwined roots in love or desire, is pure unknowing. The curious weightings of the pending string of beads hold the engaged hook and eye of the clasp taut, metal upon metal. My father's often ruinous sentimentalities and absurd dreamings are countered, held in check by the cool, sardonic appraisals of life which my mother was prone to voice. In the repertoire of their romance these oppositions show themselves.

By the early 1920s, my father was back in Brooklyn and courting my mother, who lived in what was to become the family residence, 172 Pulaski Street, a large old brownstone in a row of similar brownstones that lined Bedford-Stuyvesant's middle-class streets. This is part of a letter to my mother written by my father before they were married:

7/10/24

Martha dear,

You have requested me to write you a letter. But of what shall I write? It is not easy to one who is so closely related to you to write of the ordinary doings and happenings in life. My mind will not permit it.

As I told you yesterday, the greatest achievement in life is happiness. And the greatest happiness arrives through love. Not only love of a man

PETE AND MARTHA dining out,
Miami Beach, the late nineteen forties.

towards a woman but love of humanity, love of your fellow creatures and love of God. When I say God I do not mean an imaginary being who dwells in heaven, but I am thinking of one who dwells here on our own beautiful earth. I am thinking of you, Martha dear, of myself, of our friends, our parents, the trees, the flowers, the birds. For everything that is beautiful and good is God to me.

Perhaps I am boring you with a lot of stuff which you might call foolishness, but I cannot help myself. Life has taken a sudden turn with me. From a carefree, frivolous boy, I have changed to a serious pondering man. For Martha dear, I am in love. Perhaps I should laugh, perhaps I should cry but neither would relieve me of my feelings. I sit for hours and think, just think, of what I cannot say, for I do not know myself. For hours at a time, I ponder of ourselves, of you and myself, of our love or rather my own for you have never expressed yourself. I fear my love. I fear for the future; I fear that it came too early in life. I do not know what

I would do, I do not know what would happen if it would all come to naught. I really am worried concerning my future and yours. Perhaps all this may mean nothing to you but it means life to me . . .

As with those earlier letters from my father's merchant seaman days, I find here, in the clichéd romanticisms, nothing that is particularly false. And like those epistles from his sea voyages, I am still moved deeply by the sentiments and rediscover in the structures of such words, figures, and exempla, not merely "language" but my father's entire necessity embodied as ink on a page. Read aloud, where the naked yearning is both exposed and evanescent, they are sounds that warm the universe. Romance, romanticisms, almost the singing of a misplaced nightingale amidst those ruled and regimented streets of Bedford-Stuyvesant. And yet all these borrowings and flowery devolutions of the words lead back, and again back, to a father I always knew.

This brass ormolu of phraseology has an additional ring and a glow to it. It is the ridiculous sound of my father's decorative language pinging faintly against the modern world, unable or unwilling to join it, as was the case later when he stood amidst the roaring machinery of Rosenthal Brothers and reminded me of a lost knight on horseback buried in a city traffic jam.

Roland Barthes has observed of the love letter that it has "no tactical value: it is purely expressive"; it catches its writer at the moment of that writer's greatest vulnerability. Such a letter as my father's above reminds me of a difficult poem one has read and unpacked: after analyzing its sophisticated images and metaphors or calculating its transgressive syntax, we come, as Baudelaire reminds us concerning most great poetry, to an idea that is essentially banal or stupid: "I love you!"

"To try to write 'love'," Barthes tells us, "is to confront the muck of language: that region of hysteria where language is both *too much* and *too little*. . . ." In my father's case, as the words summon him before me, I reflect that in his character, there was very little room *not* to believe what he wrote; his deployment of the sentimental baggage of words came without irony and had less to do with a display of personality than a concession *in extremis* to his own hopes and fears.

My mother's response (if there was one) has been lost, but these excerpts, from a later letter dated June 21, 1927, and probably written while my father was travelling, give some idea of my mother's contrasting style and ironic state of mind:

Dear Pete,

Being the recipient of two of your letters today, I thought I would answer the fat one and help disillusion you on some points. However, before I do, I must tell you that you are missing a good wedding to which you might have escorted me tonight if you hadn't gone and left me. As it is, I am going with Pearl and Sam. Laugh that off!

Now I expect to take up your letter, and answer each part as it appears. I expect to make this a serial story, a page each day and when you get to Chicago, you can read the book.

What do you mean by saying I am lazy about writing? Where do you get off with that? I have always found my letter writing an immense pleasure, and delight in writing to those *at a distance*. As to my dating my letter *July* you know how fast I am; and then again I didn't expect you to get it until late in August. But I honestly must have forgotten time. . . .

What do you mean by attacking my English? I'll hit you one. I haven't started saying anything about yours because I thought I'd give you a good time. I should advise your being a bit more particular in writing or how will I be able to show my rotten letters to the girls. . . .

Such playful verbal sparring permeates the enormous correspondence over the years, much of which was saved by my mother who, perhaps, in her own fashion, saw the chance documents piling up as stays of identity against the constant brushes with death her heart trouble and cancers occasioned. If her words sassed or mildly stung, still between the lines, one read a strong current of deep feeling, as when my mother wrote to my father: "Dearest, Your galaxy of letters overwhelmed me. Four in two days, have practically smitten me off my feet, and so it took me till now to answer so much love, devotion and affection. Up to now I thought you had turned into ice water, or salt, or what not, but with the return of your bon mots, I know spring is here again."

And my father, in this epistolary duet, often exhibited the mild chastisements of my mother's wit. "Dearest Sweetheart:" he writes, "This is my fourth letter to you today. The others I have discarded. My heart is too full, and I have so much to say. Yet I'll be very brief, as I know you dislike reading my long letters."

The stylistics of these letters intrigues me. As inheritance, one could search for one's own ways of forming sentences, i.e., what borrowings and ways of shaping personal happiness or duress are embodied in the lilt of phrase or line. One would want, first of all, to see how in language a self was constructed, to see how that language was borrowed from the histories upon histories of self-presentation. For what I seem to inherit is precisely those effects that literary analysis cannot account for, the self-hidden sentimentalities and romantic tropes of my father and the ironies of my mother, ironies induced by the constant awareness of death which made her look scornfully on the hungers and complacencies of sentimentality. Such opacities absorb my thinking.

And yet, these letters are not literature. They have such innocent and obvious goals and strivings that their instrumentality almost cancels any literary effect they might have. That is, there is a side of them that is blind to the very linguistic gestures a self makes as it imprisons itself in form. We understand literature, poetry and novels, by reading into every affect of the text a recursiveness which draws us not to the invented world of the book but to the textures of words and wordings by which we are seduced. On this account, the making of literature is the least pure of our linguistic activities. Even its obvious narcissism is beclouded, doubled by the game of stylistics the literary act must play in order that it be noticed, that it not be mistaken for another kind of writing. The primal guilty conscience of every poem, beyond content or form, is that peculiarity by which it seeks recognition as poetry. My parents' correspondence, for all its show of role playing, of stances and assumptions, is in this regard less censurable. In the realm of language, it is as though between the communications of my parents and the literary tradition there is a nearly unbridgeable gap.

My mother's family, the Rosenthals, had come from Romania. From what I have been able to learn, they were of a slightly higher social stratum than my father's family, the Hellers. Rabbis, particularly those who, like my grandfather Zalman Heller, had come from the old country, were, in New York and Brooklyn in the 1920s, as plentiful as gnats in July and, personal qualities aside, about as socially elevated. The generic "reb," the spiritual creature, the student or teacher of the Old World yeshivas, had already become something of a comic figure in the *shtetls* of Poland and Russia. His otherworldliness, the misbegotten lack of the most ordinary skills, the inattentiveness to matters of washing and dress, coupled with his self-importance, had rendered him a fairly ridiculous person, especially in the eyes of hardworking mothers, wives, and sisters. In secular America, with its veneration of the commercial and utilitarian, the process of devaluation was accelerated until the rabbi was a merely a kind of spiritual Notary Public, putting an official stamp on the transactions of life swirling around him while saying little about them. From conversations with my mother I gathered that such disdain for the rabbinical class was already a part of her mother's makeup.

My mother's mother, Grandma Ernestine, as she was called, was a well-off business woman with aristocratic pretensions. She claimed titled and hereditary roots, a distant relationship to some black sheep of a Baron Rosenthal, but it was hard in my mind to connect Romanian royalty and Romanian Jewry. A domineering individual, Ernestine was bent on controlling and shaping the lives of her children. Diminutive and well dressed in the photographs I have seen of her, she appears haughty yet without display. Formality, personal dis-ease, the implications of tight-bosomed dresses held fast by lengthy rows of brass buttons, the rows of hooks for boot laces, a pince-nez or wire spectacles, these are but constellations surrounding the stern, unsmiling jut of her jaw, the psychic center of all her portraits.

In our family ruminations, unlike the names of other relatives, Grandma Ernestine's was rarely mentioned. I can think of only one or two occasions when stories of her business acumen or harshness swept through the family like a wildfire leaving behind swaths of blackened wood and the ash of resentment. Through any such talk, my mother was strangely mute, as though some unwritten law prevailed or some deep unfathomable misery coated her own tongue with those ashes.

Grandma Ernestine was already dead before I was born, but the effects of her dominance and personality, some would say karma, lived on not only in my mother's stoical toughness, but in the tragic personhood of another daughter, Gertrude, Gertie to my mother, her sister. Gertie's story is emblematic of the power of my grandmother.

Gertie, it seems, had the misfortune of falling deeply in love with someone of whom her mother, Grandma Ernestine, disapproved. When she couldn't keep the two lovers apart, when Gertie became morose or wild in her despair, my grandmother took the expedient of committing her own daughter to a mental asylum, an extreme but not totally uncommon practice of the day. Gertie never came out. Broken heart, hysteria, the proximate madness of others, an intolerable and rigid hospital staff, these must have conspired to institutionalize Gertie for the remainder of her life.

I only learned this fact many years later when I had already graduated from college and was again living in New York. Gertie, over the years, had been kept in the New York State Mental Hospital at Kings Park, Long Island. When, after I had settled in New York City and my mother came on her annual summer visits to see other family relatives, it became one of my duties to drive her to see Gertie.

Before that time, "Gertie" had only a been a word, rarely uttered and never explained, a name floating in undefined space, two syllables dribbled carelessly, as it were, from Mnemosyne's mouth into the endlessness of time without history.

Now a child is quite willing to listen to a word, as we did, for its sounds alone: *Gertie, Ger-Tee, Ger-Tee*, these struck the ear like a strange mechanical bird call or the pumping steam of a locomotive. A child, more so than an adult, will close up that void created by lack of definition by inventing complicated fantasies and imaginings, picking up ambient bits of language and binding them into odd logics of history and event. In other words, rather than adult denial or indifference, the child secretes the mysterious matter into the matrices of play or talk. Throughout my childhood, the word *Gertie* was not so "out of mind" that I didn't give her name to a bird or to a passenger on my wind-up train or set her afloat as a pebble on a leaf raft in the rain-filled gutters of Pulaski Street.

But for an adult, an undefined name makes for uneasiness. Something we sense even in the most idle of conversations when a name whose referent we can't identify is bandied about. Such discomfort has, I think, a deep historical context. A proper noun, according to the ancients, is a border, a place where the finite and infinite touch, where the chaos of the undefined has been gathered into the hard knots of language. Even today, unexplained or left hanging, a name conjures a crack in the walls of the world, a place on the back side of meaning, which suffers an exposure to the undifferentiated voids of time, to the ego's fear of anonymity and of never having lived. Such fear must lie, I think, behind our often abstracted hunger for precision, a hunger that reaches beyond either utility or aesthetics.

For the grownup Rosenthals, the word *Gertie* was the sound of family shame. Already then, by the time my mother drew me into those visits, behind the word *Gertie*, which I had heard as a child, were other words that the sounds of her name covered, words such as *madness* or *craziness* (perhaps *hate* and *love* as well). In back of *Gertie* lay a secret edifice, an oppressive sociology of parental, legal, and family matters, too upsetting for the adult Hellers and Rosenthals to contemplate. No one said her name if they could possibly avoid it; for its utterance threatened to bring all those hidden things into the open.

Naming and fear of naming. These were the poetics of those trips to Kings Park during which my mother found it extremely difficult to talk. A long habit of silence, the imprisonment of Gertie which it covered, these were subjects not easily broached between child and parent. Thus our visits to see Gertie were appallingly claustrophobic. They reduced my mother and me to the bonded mechanisms of the nuclear family, isolate persons orbiting in shameful silence about each other. Any word might open up a yawning canyon of embarrassment or guilt, for in all the years of Gertie's institutionalization, even after the death of Grandma Ernestine, no one had raised a hand or said a word to get her released. This history of silence, its shame and anguish, my memory wants to rebuke, as though silence were merely a species of forgetfulness. But, necessarily, words are formed late, usually shaped more to propel a future than indict a past. What good, I thought, to upbraid in astonished anger and horror, my own mother, who sat next to me in the car, already shrivelled in painful shame, daubing at her tears with a Kleenex. And it was also true that by the time Ernestine, the mother, died, Gertie's condition had deteriorated beyond the point where a return to normal life was possible. The mother's evil act had stood beyond her death.

So it was that on these occasions, my mother and I were trapped together in that darkened bottle-jar of familial conspiracies and invariant rituals, following the Long Island Expressway out to Kings Park as though we were attending a funeral of someone already dead, stopping first at the local Woolworths where my mother would buy some nylons and cheap cosmetics for Gertie, then next to a nearby diner to pick up some pastrami sandwiches for the two of us and Gertie to eat.

We then entered the extensive grounds of the Kings Park hospital complex with its lawns, its clumps of trees, and its walking paths along which patients wandered freely each with his or her own oddity, talking to themselves or smiling vacantly out of the puffed cheeks and hooded eyes of Mongoloid features. Our first stop was the main office where Gertie's whereabouts were checked, for she was constantly being moved from building to building depending on her condition. Toward the last of our visits, Gertie would be permanently placed in a high-security facility, one with locked doors and barred windows from which laughter and wild shriekings rent the summery air.

Most often, my mother found Gertie housed in a building from which she could be temporarily released. While I waited, my mother entered it and after awhile, the two sisters emerged to go sit on one of the benches not far from my parked car. There they had their lunch. My mother and Gertie ate together, but I had to consume my sandwich alone in the car, for it was understood that I was to be kept apart from Gertie unless my mother summoned me otherwise. The presence of a male, I was told by my mother, could heighten Gertie's emotions, causing her to claw out or run away in fear.

Gertie, a few years younger than my mother, was physically almost her double. Often she wore a cheap lightly colored dress or a striped hospital smock, the newly purchased lipstick and rouge accentuating the distraught, angular quality of her face until it was a comic visual homonym of my mother's. Occasionally, an attendant hovered nearby, as on more than one visit Gertie had become hysterical, shattering my mother's composure with pleas and entreaties to be taken away with her. Once in a rare while, my mother brought Gertie over to the car. I would step out and she would introduce us, and then I would say a few meaningless commonplaces to her. Gertie would look down at her feet or jerk her head, eyes scanning treetops or the sky. It would only be an accident if our eyes met, and then for only a second, enough time for hers to transmit an unbearable insecurity and guilt. Knowing that her own mother's actions had put her here, all I could think of was how terribly we share the earth with each other. At my mother's urgings, Gertie would tentatively shake my hand, and I would notice that both our fingers were shiny with the grease of the pastrami sandwiches. Over Gertie, the leaves on the trees moved faintly, the light and the dark playing on the quivering planes of her face. The shadows were not the past but the present pouring judgment back onto those thirty lost years.

MAMALOSHON

At night, dream sentences
That will not write themselves.

And there are phrases
You forget. Dawn comes;

It's only luck
Her breast is not your mother's.

So much touched by words,
At least you live.

What escapes makes for the grave—
A respectable marker.

Note to Mamaloshon:

The mother's speech. Language is, in a sense, identifiable with the voice, the cooing of the mother who is always desired and always unattainable. Our need for language is rooted in our need to summon what is outside ourselves, what is other, what is different.

From Scholem's Kabbalah: *The kabbalistic idea of* parzutim, *literally "physiognomies" or "faces," represents the central manifestation of primordial man in which all the positive and negative aspects of man and creation are intermixed. But the intermixture is also held in opposition because some aspects are masculine, others female, hence they become renamed as* Abba *and* Imma, *"father and mother." Scholem tells us that divergence and separateness are the medium for reindividuation and redifferentiation of all beings "into transmitters and receivers of influx." The division into sexes is the precondition for procreative coupling, for "looking face-to-face which is the common root of all intellectual and erotic unions."*

Yet, if, as Harold Bloom remarks, "the unconscious turns out alas not to be structured like a language but to be structured like Freud's language," then, following Freud, the poet's relation to the language of dream, especially erotic dream, is also a "family romance." Poetry, like the discourse of the psychoanalyst, or in the very act of taking up "the family," finds itself both outside and beside *the things it would frame or comment on. Mother and child-man. Every recognition of a psychic bind, because it is knowledge, weakens the infant's empowering of language and strengthens language's adult side, its mature desiring. Language can undo itself, delivering us to the real-life lover, but at the cost of delivering us into Time, the awareness of which is an adult awareness entailing one's own death. Such recognition is the poem's tension and* potentia.

And yet, behind this tension is the most ancient phantasy of "secret" languages and even of those available languages not yet personally known (I know no Yiddish). This phantasy involves an occultic view of language, one that would tranform its metaphoric or metonomic suggestiveness into an instrumentality, no longer merely wishing but wish fulfilling.

My parents were married twice, first, as though my mother had learned the lesson of Gertie well, after a secret elopement. Then again in the fullness of convention's customs on Saturday, June 23rd, 1928, as evidenced by the gold-printed wedding announcement which appears to have less to do with the celebration of a certain kind of event than with the profferings, the sumptuousnesses, of the caterer, Sam Dornstein (his name appears in the largest type on the announcement): a full seven course meal from Appetizer: "Pineapple Surprise" through Relishes, Fish, Soup, Entree, Roast, Dessert, and Beverages. The proceedings are held in Temple Ohel Moshe Chevre Thilim at Willoughby and Tompkins Avenues, an intersection not far from our Pulaski Street house. The only memory I have of that synagogue, which was still in use while I lived in Brooklyn, is a vague one, connected with the fasting on the Day of Atonement.

"Can the human word," Gershom Scholem writes, "contain the word of God in its pure form, or can the word of God, if it exists, express itself within the confines of the human language?" The answer, for me, to both of these questions can only be yes. Any attempt to separate God word and human word would have no meaning or force whatsoever. This idea is one that could hold true whether one were a believer or not. Or to phrase it in Scholem's words, the Absolute is recognizable by the infinite number of interpretations that can be brought to it. The poem is then not an act of naming but of renaming; as Blake saw it: not generation, but regeneration. What is prime, the causal factor of the poem, is the world, the unnameable angel who is struggled with, in order to find the blessed name, Israel, the place of God or divinity. This much I allow myself.

More troubling in their complexity to me were the structurings of the divine word, as in Genesis with its designation of God as first speaker. Or, as in the Gospel of John and in the Kabbalist's Torah where Word and Letter are originary and precede God, for here, the divine Speaker reads from Creation's prepared script, naming off the universe's essential constituents as he creates them: "Let there be Light," "Let the waters under the heaven be gathered," etc. "God said" and "God called:" these are instrumentalities and not communications, ways of sound-ing and matter-ing we can barely conceive. The graphs and calculations by which, from a kind of impossible nothingness, the Cosmos is invented, the summings and entanglements lost in First Causes and diddlings of the ineffable, leap off our mental curves and refuse any contemplative willing.

And isn't there something, too, of the madman or anxious worrier, the neurotic artist, in this God who speaks to whom but himself? Who perhaps cannot bear the otherness of His own actions and brings them to familiarity by voice-overs upon his own gestures and creations? And who makes humans (as humans make love or works of art) because, ultimately, solipsism is unbearable?

Therefore Adam. God pauses in the linguistic realm, in the hidden, secret sabbath, not of rest, but of primal words. He will listen to his Creation, watch it play out. He is curious, for instance, to see how Adam will name the animals—well and good, the names are allowed to stand. Thus, one causal reading of the Bible's first chapter might claim that free will's origin lies in God's weariness with self-reflexivity, in the burden of speaking and hearing alone. And that it is in His speculations, in his possible bemusement with the permissions of language let loose upon the things of the world, that his interest in His creation is rekindled.

Here, too, long before Nietzsche, is the beginning of God's undoing. From the earliest moments of creation, the desire to be released from the dread and boredom of the solipsistic, to acknowledge or give sanction to a world not solely one's own, undercuts sacred authority. Adam and Eve, apple, tree, language, serpent, these begin the undermining. Spirituality now belongs not to the literalists and fundamentalists but to the rebellious, to the province of heresy, to those who will bring down the prison house of authority and authoritativeness. Only fearful priests and those with totalitarian mindsets would still hold God and man in the old prison of literalism, which is to say that these religious fascists arrogantly identify their own minds with the Absolute.

I would add that the anthropomorphic presumptuousness of this formulation I have given above is only another version of the poet's story, one that could probably be stated without the name of any supernatural agency.

But continuing with this causal tale, *Word* is now, suddenly, word, something intercommunicative; how else to warn man and woman of earthly things, of a tree or a serpent? And it is word, in this story of creation, that sets things in motion, but not to run like a machine. Rather, the energy of the world courses through, is based on difference, on variant and contestation, on the dance of thingness and creatureliness. Human word and name, these predicating acts, are now local forms of God's kinetic asseverations, ways of making things happen. The sacred (if it can be known at all) and the secular are posited not on the literal name, but on the act of naming.

Proper names in the Bible, scholars have suggested, are not merely tags of identity but receptacles of character and personality. Name imposes shape, becomes a focus point or location by which the world is subjectively construed. The integrity of personality is constrained, is enveloped or cupped in the denomination. As Adam founds human language he also founds forms and ingatherings. Each specificity is a demarcation, *this* and not *that*. The ultimate seat of individuality resides in one's name.

A syllable was added to my grandfather's name; Zalman became Solomon. For the American English prosodist, an additional beat, a minor problem with the ordering of time (or its rhyme). For my grandfather, the modifications to his name initiated a re-orienting and re-ordering of space, of Europe to America. Still, behind that re-ordering, in the abutments of letter to letter, syllable to syllable, the potential unity of his being, as a principle of organization, was implicitly maintained.

But I think now, not of that revised name's mere syllabic differentiating sound, but of an adjacency of names, not of revision but of addition, of something like *Mike the Kike*.

"Kike." I must have always known what this word means. I was eleven or twelve, and the bus pulled up to the corner of Washington Avenue and Lincoln Road, downtown Miami Beach, where I was waiting and began to disgorge its mostly elderly passengers, some with canes or with tremors who gingerly tested, as though it were an alpine trail, the steps leading down to the curb.

If I project, the image is suddenly biblical. The elderly, garbed like so many Josephs, are wearing multicolored resort wear; they mumble in the speech inflections of the world, guttural and poignant. The corner where the bus stops is Miami Beach's only business district with its few tall buildings, smooth and hard, housing offices. A large digital clock on the First Federal Bank building rules the time and space of these pillars of Moloch. They have come, these aged citizens, from rest and leisure, from the tidal littorals of brilliant light and sand or from dark close-to-death naps in cool apartment rooms, to cash their social security and pension checks, to wander among the markets and clothing stores of South Beach.

Among those getting off the bus, a young man in a seersucker suit, a tie, who turns to his young wife, she in white gloves and pearls—Midwesterner tourists?—and says, loud enough for me to hear, "These kikes are slow."

What is epithet or slur? In my astonished fury, this I know, when I heard "kike" uttered, it became my word. That is, the name "Mike" was not simply revised to become "Michael" or "Mikey" (my childhood friend's occasional variant). Instead, "Mike" was suddenly carrying an added weight, an additional tag of a name imposed from outside and known to be from outside by the article *the*, the word *kike* and the spaces between words. The name I had never wanted was now mine, suddenly etched or branded, as conventional wisdom would have it, not only to the other names by which I was called but to me. To one's name, an identity-centering sound, was suddenly appended an eccentric weight, a clumsy metallic lump of negative sound and meaning which, as though destroying the balance of a wheel, threatened to pull the structure of one's being apart. More than a transmutation of one's self, the unwanted name, the stigmatization for which I would have to compensate, had revised and transformed the world this self sees.

SOME ANTHROPOLOGY

And yet poems remind me of the tribe of the gentle Tasaday who some regard merely as members of another tribe taught to fool anthropologists with false primitiveness and *naivete*, to be blunt in their manners and infernally innocent. No one is sure, as with poems, whether they are real or a hoax, whether the dictator, in his munificence, created a forest preserve to shelter them as he might set aside an apartment for a poet in the palace. Forests and palaces, such utopias are mostly exclusionary, like hotels for the rich, and needn't concern us. It is rainy for a rain forest to house our myths, to shelter our lost tribes, who, one by one, gather in a clearing. I sometimes think about my lost tribe of Jews, American Jews, also part hoax and part invention, whose preserve is sheltered under brick where limousines hum and one hears the faint, familiar babble of the homeless. As it happens, the Tasaday are being declared "non-existent" by government scientists so their hardwood forests can be transformed into chests of drawers. Strange, then, the anthropology of the poet who must build his poems out of the myths he intends to falsify, who says, look my friend, you are laying away your laundered shirts in a rain forest.

Note to Some Anthropology:

Cf. The New York Times, *January 30, 1988, Letters to the Editor, "What's Behind Strange Tasaday Hoax Charges": "As for the T'boli [another tribe of the Phillipines] who say they were paid to be Tasaday, remember the poverty. Give me a ticket to Mindanao and a couple of hundred bucks and I will produce 500 T'boli who say they are the Congress of the United States."—Kaa Byington.*

I consider myself a reasonably robust person, enjoying food, wine, sex, music, the pleasures of hiking in the mountains or of following aimless *wanderjahrs* in the large cities of the world. All my subliminal terrors are associated with my father who died in the babblement of Alzheimer's or Parkinson's disease—we in the family were never sure which took over in the end. For this reason, I am alarmed when I discover that I too much resemble him. My unconscious mimicry of his gestures, the way he thought, with his hand on his chin or plucked at his ear as he spoke, inspire me with fear. What physical rules govern the poetics of remembrance? Is there, in something beyond fear or understanding, a reverse physics of onomastics? Can a Michael revert to a Peter, a process of un-naming?

Memory with its strange frightening tricks: I often imagine I'm merely labelling my own ways and doings as "like" his, a way of preparing for one's own aging and death, of inventing a rationale for what can't be comprehended. Documents would help, photographs—but who would photograph his father in his moments of weakness and vulnerability?

And suddenly, I am remembering one of the most ambivalent objects I have made, that watercolor of my father in his decline which now hangs on the wall in the room where I am writing this. I painted it only a few months before he actually entered a nursing home, and here, amid the lightly washed-in backgrounds of furnishings and walls, my father naps in his easy chair, his feet on a hassock, his hands over his thighs, hanging limply as I often find my own hands when I am rest. In my fitful unease, I can imagine a transfer, a kind of bodily receptivity that suggests that the things we make with our hands, our eyes and heart, can also become part of our bodily makeup. "Signs," Julia Kristeva writes, "are what produce a body . . . symbolic production's power [is] to constitute *soma*." With every stroke of the brush, with every lingering, in poem or text, upon the being of my father, I have haunted his existence into mine.

So when I sit at the desk and write or think, when I imagine a dialogue undertaken, a letter to be written, a communication with someone else, when I visualize these things, I see also my father at his desk. I sit his way, I bend over the surface of the desktop, I look down at the paper or the typewriter as he did. I feel, in the composite set of my muscles, in the position of my bones, the ready, wistful irony of his own communications, as though I were living in a curiously vibrating world, *me . . . him, me . . . him, me . . . him.* This vibrational space is larger than our individual existences, larger than the psychologist's view of parental influence, larger than the genotyping of generation upon generation. It seems to me that at any moment all of what exists can be put into question, that an identity crisis is continually at the mind's border, particularly concerning the meanings of reality, but that in this questioning one passes, not over, but through all of one's personal and collective histories rather like a needle piercing many layers of fabric. It is not blank, open space that one moves into, but a space populated by all one knows, knowledge, event.

Memory, as Umberto Eco writes, becomes "the shadow of order," and order is the syntax of the universe. This is how I live in my father's shadow, not in fear of him, but that I *am* him.

The word of God and the human word. Contemplating these, I suffer an irony. All naming and renaming, in our spiritual progressions, lead onward to one name, that of God, which, strictly speaking, is unnameable. A curious circle: the arc of a life begins in the imperfect babble of the child. Later, we learn to speak, to shape predicates of being. In that speaking inheres the possibility of human and psychic growth which leads again to speechlessness—not that of death which is the end of growth but to an awe and strict reverence. We perhaps, unwarrantably, elevate the laconic person. His or her silence before adversity displays not lack but a surfeit of knowledge. Loquaciousness marks the fool or the anxious person, not someone to lead you out of Hell. But the wise ones, in their silence, counsel plenitude.

One formula: poetry is condensation, is language moving toward its own nonexistence. As a poet's words seek an Eliotic "impersonality," sounding themselves almost against what is purely subjective or private, as they fight to become universal, the very thing they struggle with is their own particularized voicing. Buried in the voice, in the physiology of throat and larynx, is what can only be the accidentals of individuation, the voiceprint (as we sense in the new security systems) of what belongs only to the poet. In order for the universal to be reached, the uttered or written word must find that voicelessness which Benjamin cryptically and paradoxically spoke of as "pure language—which no longer means or expresses anything but is, as expressionless and creative Word, that which is meant in all languages."

The words and images of a poem are laconic figures in just the way of the wise. Dense poetic compactions, as in Emily Dickinson or in Sappho or in the struggles *not to speak,* as in Paul Celan's minute German syllabaries (where every bit of language recalls to him that the *Shoah* is constructed of German): these are great magnets or black holes of human possibility. They don't make a world; they gather it and, for a moment, in their immense specific gravity, hold all its articulations.

So too, our histories and memories come in such potent fragmentary instances, in weighted and isolate images and pictures, each one capable of surmounting all of a world like a crown set on a mountain peak. We are not merely remembering, but like blind persons and their braille, we feel the raised surfaces of a glyph.

What, I ask myself, constitutes my un-belief? As I put what I deem my aspirations, what I would rise to, under scrutiny, I maintain that certain lineaments of my life—of any life—are, if not theological, at least somewhat religious. One is surrounded by the heaven and hell of the modern city, by the intense glamor and seductiveness of its people and its shops, even by the foetus-like curls of street people asleep in doorways, by the bent and unhappy riders of subways. These things are, for good or ill, an incitement to wakefulness, even if it be to repel the image of the foul bum or to lust for the city's sexual beings or exotic foods. What is religious, after all, are the very things that question the boundaries of our being, that enable a traverse of psychic chasms, of difference and otherness. Thus, I find in this "awake" quality the meaning of Jacob Neunser's remark that "Judaism rejoices at the invitation of the secular city." The modern city is a concentrate of what Eastern religious thought calls "attachment." And without this world, without its *samsaric* barb (to continue with non-Western terminologies) there is no *nirvana*, no wisdom without confusion. So, too, with language. Without silence there is no language, but also, without babble (Babel), we have no movement from the confused and unintelligible toward legibility and articulation.

Did the secular as a category even exist for my grandfather? Asleep, in a sense, in his assured and monotonous recitation of the *Haggadah*, my grandfather seemed to efface not only the exact sense of ritualistic Word but the counterpointing silence by which the ritual meaning becomes articulate. Belief, for him, was an attained realm, a certainty of being in consonance with some divine principle rather than a matter of faith to be moment by moment realized.

My mother who did not believe in God, who told me this fact when I was only nine as we lolled in the shallow waves off the beach at Lummis Park. My mother who said "I am an atheist" under the clearest of

MY MOTHER dressed up for a fancy costume
ball, Miami Beach, the nineteen fifties.

blue skies, when not the merest wisp of haze or cumulus lay in the way between heaven and earth:

My mother, who suffered numerous illnesses, a series of different cancers, a bad heart, and finally a death-dealing stroke, my mother, who yet outlived three of her doctors and led an active and social life, who had closets of dresses, who walked with dignity up steps, taking ten seconds to rest at each landing, this mother was immensely proud of her teeth. In the morning and in the evening, she spent many minutes in the bathroom flossing and brushing; at night, while we children lay in bed, we could hear her gargling. My mother pestered the butcher for soup bones which she would boil up, not for soup, but to chew on. My mother, who was very conscious of her appearance and so dressed smartly and even elegantly on most occasions, would sit by herself at the dining room table in the late afternoons with a large billowing napkin tucked into the neck of her housedress and gnaw like a dog on those cooked bones. When out having lunch with a friend or with us, she always excused herself at the end of a meal and retired to the ladies' room to brush her teeth. How astonishing her pride in those teeth while the rest of her body was failing her.

On the Day of Atonement, when the litany of Jewish suffering is recited in the synagogue and as a young child, just after the Second World War aware of the Holocaust, and feeling the entire world massed against Jews, feeling my own vulnerability, when the rest of the family engaged in the ritual fasting, in bringing neither liquid nor food to one's lips and mouth, my mother, because of her health, was required to eat, and so, required herself to brush her teeth. In the Temple, surrounded by all the fasting relatives and family friends, in a cloud of bad breath, only my mother's mouth as she kissed me had any sweetness.

PALESTINE

I.

Snow glides down in the west Forties.
Like a child, I could lick the snowflakes
from my wrists. In storms,
bums will nibble at the wood of tenement doorways.
The weather precipitates dreams, fantasies, I too

have my dreams of the snow's purity,
of its perfecting worlds, so little like my own.
Could I be a gentleman of this snow, my calling card
one evanescent flake to place upon a blemish?

Frankly, I'm delighted with a new scientific proof:
at any moment at least two places on the globe
must experience similar weather. Hence my
Palestine and hence my joy. Baudelaire
watched the Negress in the street stomp her feet
and imagine date palms. I don't want the territory,
just the intensity of a visit. Sh'ma Yisrael, only
the symbol world holds you and me or I and Thou.
Sh'ma Palestine, aren't you always where snow falls.

II.

My Palestine, which means I love one woman,
so why not two? Which means I love that distant sky
and the lovely irritants of my inner eye. My tears
for what in life is missed. The Red Sea of my philosophy
will irrigate with salt these barren lands.

Does snow fall there too?

III.

Always somewhere else, and always held by someone else . . .
Sweet figs, sweet thighs to Suez or Port Said.
But when snow falls one's place is yet another place.

IV.

In that salty biblical sweetness, why avenge?
Grief is vectored north, east, west, the Wailing Wall.
Why avenge? Terror has cast its rigid mask,
and with fraternal semblance, transformed all
into sisters and brothers. Why avenge?
Only the dead wear human faces.

V.

Yea, though I am not lifted out of sorrow,
yea, though the opus of self-regard endoweth me
for nearly nothing, I have not forgotten snow. I
have no more forgotten snow than other poets forget
time or blackbirds. I have, with love, put the snow aside,
I have let the snow melt so that I may envision Judea
as a stately gentile lady, a crusader, a crusade.

VI.

I am so far away,
yet for Americans
distances are musical.
So I am near. I am with snow
which softens the city in which I live.
I am in the Forties and the snow glides down
and fills all the niches that lie between
the living and the dead.

Note to Palestine:

Vide. *"Accidental Meeting With an Israeli Poet" and the note for that poem.*

Also, to the onomastics of renamed nations, to combined and divided loyalties by which the poet becomes historical witness. Jew/American. Israel/Palestine. The world does not correspond to, even escapes from, one's attempts to pin it down to language. Man the language user is man the inevitable creature of dualisms.

Even as a "political" poem strives to rise above its occasion sub specie aeternitatis, *it must speak in the language of historical particulars, it must redeem each day, as Benjamin put it, as though it were the Day of Judgment. The truth of our judgment days, the end of our days on earth, brings with its biblical message, the actuality of our human temporality, the finality and even frustration of having thought we owned something, most of all a land. And yet, if my "Palestine" is full of dualities of place, of names and of intentions, yet, as with the weather theory which I found discussed in the* NY Times, *there must be places far apart which are joined by similar psychic "weathers," mentalities, and sympathies—poetry would seem to be based upon them—which would then open channels for mutual understanding and cessation of violent struggle. Possession need not go much further. Against that view is the specter of a final struggle in which death joins all humanity in a night of silence.*

"Section VI": Isaac Rosenfeld, American literary and music critic, remarked that Americans loved the themes of exile and alienation because for them "all distances are musical."

Memory as a process of making things legible in this sense: our lived time is not only that which we have left trailing behind us, but the shaping force which moves us forward. The forces, the myths that enclose us and hence escape our consciousness, often seem natural or givens of one's life. When I reflect, glimpsing the structure of my own mythology, a future suddenly appears not as a blank but as something configured of vestigial hopes, fears, dreads. My past and future are in communication, speaking somewhere over my head, and so, as I write out my past into sentences (which indeed they are, both grammatically and judgmentally), I discover in the economy of temporality that the past and the future have conspired together, to write me over again, to engender themselves and myself as a speck of eternal recurrence. And yet that which is made legible by the act of writing can be erased, modified, rewritten, elided. To remember is to invoke the hidden syntax of continuity and by that have some power to disrupt it.

ACCIDENTAL MEETING WITH AN ISRAELI POET

At the playground by the Con Ed plant,
this is strange: from tall brick stacks,
smoke is bleeding off into cloudless sky.
Little dreams, little visions must go like that.

Still, his boy and mine play in their soccer game,
each move, each kick or run precise and self-
contained. From one end of the field to the other

they go, from sun to deep shade. And there's no
poof, no gone, no fade into that all-capping blue.
Trampled ground, grass, sun-tinged webs of cable—

so this is how we reckon hope, as something
blotted up by matter that it might better
circulate in brick, in the squared-off shadows

of the powerplant to commingle with children
and with games and sides, with wire and with steel
until, lo, the helmet of a soldier has sopped it up!
It sits there, insisting on a certain rightness.

And yet people's songs disperse into the air,
people's songs and rhetoric . . .

Note to Accidental Meeting with an Israeli Poet:

The poet of this poem is Yehuda Amichai, who was a visiting professor at New York University where I teach, and whose son played on the same soccer team as mine. The subtext of the poem is the ambivalent reality of Israel and the dilemma of thousands of years of Jewish history having culminated in a Promised Land having material as well as spiritual being.

In Midrashic literature, certain anecdotes and stories are referred to as "king parables," parables in which the central figure is a king who is likened to a Roman Emperor. The minor characters of the parable, dominated by the ruler, are his court and army. The soldier in the poem, acting under the warrant of the imperial state, seems like one of these dominated characters. Imperial fiat, power blinded to everything else but its goal, seems antithetical to the spirit of a Peoples' song, and to poetry with its cultivation of hope even amidst suffering and ambivalence.

Amichai's own work, in particular, seems to capture the contradictory flavor of this dilemma, as in these verses of his short poem, "An appendix to the vision of peace":

> *Don't stop after beating the swords*
> *into ploughshares, don't stop! Go on beating*
> *and make musical instruments out of them.*

> *Whoever wants to make war again*
> *will have to turn them into ploughshares first.*

George Steiner, in "Our Homeland, The Text," writes: "To experience
Torah and Talmud as *mikra*, to apprehend these texts as cognitive and

emotional plenitude, is to hear and accept a summons." The written homeland, and yet one creates or hears the incarnate being making an utterance in the recitation of the text, in its orality. How to understand this? If the text is written down, made codifiable, then it emulates, not the performative collocations of the poet-bard, but the in-errant word of God, a deeper matter. It retains its oral character, but finds this orality in each individual instance of reading. Thus it fulfills the other demand of Creation: that it be interpreted, that it come down, ultimately, to structurations as language.

The physiology of writing, as Father Walter Ong suggests, is bracketed by aloneness. "I am writing a book," he comments, "which I hope will be read by hundreds of thousands of people, so I must be isolated from everyone. While writing the present book, I have left word that I am 'out' for hours and days—so that no one, including persons who will presumably read the book, can interrupt my solitude." Such solitude is often an aspect of spirituality. Isaac of Acre, the thirteenth-century Spanish Kabbalist, writes: "He who is vouchsafed the entry into the mystery of adhesion to God, *devekuth*, attains to the mystery of equanimity, and he who possesses equanimity attains to loneliness, and from there he comes to the holy Spirit and to prophecy." In this passage, one can identify not only a sacred journey of the soul but also a kind of *poesis*, for to come "to prophecy" means ultimately to come to speech, to poetry, to utter both hope and dread. The loneliness that Isaac of Acre speaks of is thus, to my mind at least, deeply connected not only to the severity and isolation of the spiritual journey but to the often wearying aloneness from which the poetic act seems to spring.

The poets who first nurtured my growth in poetry—I think here of the Jewish Objectivists, of Charles Reznikoff, of George Oppen, Carl Rakosi, and Louis Zukofsky—struck me as being married to their aloneness, as to a bride. Little noticed by the public or the academy, they wore the public neglect of their work as prideful badges. These were the poets whose books I carried on my own *hegira*, my wanderings, as I tried to find the forms my words and acts must take and be taken for.

Reznikoff, in particular, was a Jewish *flâneur*, a diminutive figure in dark suit and tie, and yet, an isolato endlessly walking the streets of the city, milling with its crowds or divagating into the suburbanlike precincts of Flatbush and outer Queens but always sensing his apartness. "I am alone—and glad to be alone," he writes in his poem "Autobiography: New York," linking himself both with the diasporic witness of an alienated consciousness and with those moments of the Jewish mystical tradition, as expressed in Isaac of Acre's words above, that acknowledge a fundamental and unbridgeable separation of God and man, but yet allow man to glimpse God, momentarily, as it were. Perhaps Reznikoff espied God on a sidewalk in Brooklyn, espied Him sardonically as kind of urban modern *deus absconditus* when he writes: 'This pavement barren/as the mountain/ on which God spoke to Moses—/suddenly in the street/shining against my legs/the bumper of a motor car." Or possibly Reznikoff experiences the religious moment as truly fleeting, like that instant of deep love in a poem of Baudelaire's when the poet sees and rapturously falls for a woman who passes quickly on the street, is swallowed up by the city, never to be seen again.

What I felt from these poets who taught me so much was the happenstance of authorship, the penetration by the world into our would-be discursiveness, our self-involved chatter.

The gloss of eyes across and over streets, as though the city were made of languages, inscribed in the ages and designs of buildings, in the oddities and samenesses of people one passed. . . . A collection of languages, written and rewritten. From so much utilitarian secularity, one might derive a nontheological sense of language, as if to say: thank Whoever (ironically of course) or whatever has designed this world. For I find new languages daily; I find that not all is written out, and that therefore I too am allowed to speak and write.

Further, there are, in the life of the writer, those moments of being sickened with one's own work, one's very words. At such times, I have risen from my desk and hurled myself out into the city, evicted myself from the precincts of my own logorrhea, partly as break or diversion, but also to be in touch with the languages of others. Thus, to gloss, to go over, as an eye savoring the textures of the world, is also to be compelled into utterance, and so to provide interlinears and commentaries.

Commentary, therefore, is first eyes before words, a searchlight of eyes on texts which invoke disturbances and consonances in the reader. Commentary, too, is never synonymous with the text; it always remains apart. And so it stands, in the idealized version of interpretation, in *devekuth*ic relation to the text. The commentary adheres to the text, and—whatever its virtues as a text in its own right—never enters into mystical union (one in the other) with it. George Oppen, in his late poems, expressed such adhesions as a kind of poetic radiation. He identified the poet as a lighthouse turned back on the coast, searching out the edges of the continent, illuminating the particular commonness of Americans, and ultimately of humans, as figures of differentiation, as ways of acknowledging the fundamental conditions of apartness. His entire poetic oeuvre was for me an endless efflorescence, a singular linguistic act of the truth of boundaries and boundedness, not only on the level of nations—where the inability to tolerate aloneness was most destructive in our time—but on the level of the singularity of individuals and on the level of consciousness relating to the nonhuman world. It was out of such often wearying aloneness that the poetic act seemed to spring.

IV

$\mathcal{A}$S A CHILD, I had gasped on, swallowed and spit up the Atlantic, the very ocean that, in its physical and psychic deliverance of them to the New World, had corroded and etched away the Old World life of my father's side of the family. Now, the taste and smell of that sea sometimes functions like Proust's *madeleine*; it not only calls up memories but inflicts a feeling of difference and separation upon me.

In Miami, on Miami Beach, on the scattered pine clumps of sand dotting Biscayne Bay, one is never far from that saltiness which psychically mingles blood and ocean with the depredations of time, with the wearing away of man-made things such as stone works and metals.

And yet, as a fairly new and speedily erected vacation place, Miami Beach also seemed constructed to repel time, to assert with Ozymandian arrogance the power of Works over the eons. For the constant peculiar islandedness of the area embossed its resort culture with the raised lips of the pleasantly fantastic and the commercially viable but improbable. It detached it as well from history and even reality. That sense of time passing, as marker and reshaper of human existence, had here been totally abandoned.

In effect, time, the causal element of all contrasts, was missing, and this led to a kind of free play of the signifiers. It gave to the shops on the streets and the hotels and swimming pools a quality of both distance and familiarity highly original to the tourist. One suspects there were other places like it in the world, certain amusement parks such as Tivoli in Copenhagen, or the cluttered *haut bourgeois* sitting rooms of Hapsburg Vienna. Yet nowhere had histories and cultures been so thoroughly ransacked, to be reconfigured on purely different (commercial) lines as in the Miami Beach hotel lobby. There, an imaginary axe had been taken to the historical-cultural continuum. Time and geography had been chopped up into eighteenth-century Chinese lacquered screens, Italian provincial settees resting on the patterned curlicues of Persian carpets where they were positioned in the shadows of plaster Venus de Milos. Strauss waltz music played on the Musak, webbing the entire lobby in the straining strands of violins. There was nothing second-rate about these fakes cleverly deployed across vast expanses of thick, dark carpet among which the Jews of the Bronx and Brooklyn and Philadelphia oohed and aahed. These tourists had come here to be provincial in a different way, both to stand in mild awe at their surroundings and to snub, with crude manners, this plaster cornucopia of the past.

Looked at from the vantage point of the present in which I write, Miami Beach was one of the original postmodern constructs, a place, an exemplar, ahead of our age in cite-ability and in working out the transformation of time from an endlessly receding background hum into a kind of symphony orchestra which played only the Sixty Greatest Moments of the music of history. Today, if one has difficulty recognizing the true originality of this pastiche, it is only because the rest of the nation has had its own consciousness raised by the media and politicians into a similar multi-chronicled simultaneity. That tattered and flaking city, the Miami Beach of my youth, lives on as exemplary simulacrum. For what more closely emulated the entrained milieus of the Fountainbleau Hotel lobby of the nineteen fifties than the absurdly juxtaposed pomposities, visual and verbal, of the Reagan presidency, of the entire decade of the Eighties?

O my people! I find it instructive that both Miami Beach and Hollywood, American dream machines *par excellence*, were in the main, products of post-immigrant Jewish consciousness. Both machines were (and still are) in the business of manufacturing occult paradises, instantly obtainable on demand. I use the word *occult* to signify something supernatural, i.e., unearned by dint of learned experience or transformations of the soul. Rather, I'm thinking of something almost too ready-to-hand, as if one had a magical key or secret oath to unlock our desires—in the case of America that oath being something like "money talks." In Miami Beach, occultation meant that the rich cultural properties of the world hung like gorgeous draperies between the world and the self, their roots in cause and effect severed by magical expediency. The magical words, the rubbed lamp, the pocketfuls of green dollars, were transports to paradisaical pleasures. Revelation on the cheap, so to speak. How contrary this place seemed to the deepest strains of Jewish religious thought where revelation is achieved, not by paying attention to the world, but by paying heed, by interpreting the text. The Miami Beach dream machines converted the world into a fantastical text, a fabric, where paradise was bought with an admission ticket or a hotel reservation at the Eden Roc.

I had been transported to Florida, to this time-bending phantasmagoria, during that crucial phase of life where one is in transition from childhood to adolescence, where one marks out distinctions between oneself and others. But as I think back, the strongest memories I have of Miami Beach, of the white hotels floating over the water, remind me that I was no more than a piece of flotsam cast up on a sea coast of illusions manufactured by someone else.

It was as though the bright sun and the sea had begun to bleach out memories of Brooklyn, to leave me rootless and alone under the wideness of the skies and the expanse of water. And thus it felt—as though it were the function of this playground of adults—that a young person like myself had been given over to a fate wholly external to himself. Such a feeling had much to do with my temperament, possibly the temperament of all uprooted children. But it also had to do with all my awareness of difference, social, financial, status, friends, intellectual, in short, the entire calculus of a young person's life transplanted into a new environment. Almost from the first days in Florida, I knew that something about my existence prior to this point was entirely over with. So now, the envisioning of this oceanic field of memory often comes back as a compounding of rust flakes or ashes stirred into life-giving water.

The processes that work on a child are in the realm of magic, embedded in a particular word and the resonance or aura the word casts, in its telling and reading. For the adult, this magic is attenuated, for the word often simply designates an object. Still, in the hands of someone skilled with words, the object's blunt face, the pain or wonder it might invoke, is doubly enhanced by voice with its timbre or by the page's stylistic flutter.

The Bible, on the other hand, in its uncertain authorship (or in the popular view of it as God's word), presents a stylistics beyond style; before the text, we are unsure what design it has on us, what it asks of our beliefs and our behavior. In this regard, as I think about my own writing, the biblical stories are the source of primary matter, of a quality even more strange and powerful than those "navels" of memory I have described above. Consider this arbitrary swirl of story and image: Adam's rib from which God made Eve; the apple bitten in the Garden; the returning dove, a twig in its beak signalling land to Noah; Jonah's whale; the Ark, which touched, struck down the defiler and was builded of shittim wood and ram's skins, with overlays of gold, with borders and candlesticks and bowls in the shape of almonds; sword hilts; spears; unmoving suns; roses and the burning bush; dogs and asses; Amalek's body hewed to pieces—the array is endless. Such arrays seem to make the Bible, more than anything else, into a poetics in which names of things form monuments of hope and fear, of sacred potentialities. Unlike Adam's earliest namings, which preceded the Expulsion and so held the pristine flavor of Creation, the piled-up objects of the narratives—after Eden, after the Fall, and after Babel—fashion themselves into honor codes and chastisements, which from the poet's point of view, resemble rubble around a building site. In such a way, the musical character of the words as speech carries over into connotations that throw colors and shadows over everything human. Certain words *are* worth far more that the thousand pretty images of the homily. They fall into the soul like stones into a deep well, into dark nether regions of the psyche, or they burst forth like springs from the rocks in brilliant torrents.

For a child, there were dreaded vocabularies surrounding my sick mother, words and phrases that formed an interlinear to the family's trials and sojourns. Fearful speech was studded with such words as *doctor*, *heart*, or *pills*. The word *silence* made me want to cry out, and terms such as *pulse rate* and *suppressed breathing* were drawn painfully out of some horrifying blackness, rib-tightening and throttling as they were enunciated. Whatever they conjured in the mind gleamed malevolently as though chipped out of basalt or onyx. I knew they were Northern words, New York and Brooklyn ones, made of heartless cement and winter. Other words, such as *Florida*, *coconuts*, *sea*, or *mother*, as they had come up in conversation in our Brooklyn dining room, were the organ stops of a Bach-like fugue of hopeful anticipations. And by the time we were living in Miami Beach, these words were to disperse their energies in a crescendo of charmed colorations.

My father had found an apartment for my mother in the Hudson Arms, a white cube of a building on 15th Street near Washington Avenue, and it was to that place that I was delivered by the Schusterhoffs, the people who brought me to Florida.

After the long rows of grim brownstones which lined Brooklyn's Pulaski Street, their bleak countenances leaning over onto the sidewalks where my friends and I played, the low Art Deco apartment houses of Miami Beach painted in creamy pastels had the appearance of giant play blocks. They were nestled among exotic trees, palms and eucalyptus, in what looked like gift baskets of writhing green excelsior. So violently alive was this plant life of South Florida that it threatened to consume the fringes of dirt and even the footings of the buildings where they met the ground. The Hudson Arms, like so many other buildings on 15th Street, sat in beds of tuberous milkweed bushes and flowering hibiscus. Jasmine plants with minute red flowers twined toward the windows of the lower floors. The local gardeners were constantly trimming back the plants, cutting and snipping until they drew out weird topiary effects, transforming branches and clusters of leaves so that they resembled animals with their claws grasping at the buildings. For a child, the flowering plants were hideaways and secret pockets of shade, light-mottled tunnels that adult eyes could not spy into and where childhood rituals such as the casting of old chicken bones like an oracle or the throwing of pen knives took place.

And how strange and interesting it felt to rub the outer walls of these buildings, the fingers coming away with a pale white powder. Later, I was to learn how to smear it on my face the way warriors smear ashes on their faces and to scare away much smaller children.

Also fixed in my memory, and unusual too because in Brooklyn one didn't find such things, was the sight of the thick pipes painted with a silver finish which delivered cooking gas to the apartment houses. Everywhere in Miami Beach these pipes elbowed up out of the cement of back alleys and parking lots and into the walls of buildings, their dull brilliance ebbing and flaring with the changes in the sky, with the movement of clouds before the sun. Resting one's hand on the pipe, one could feel the faint vibrations of the gas as it travelled into buildings. Even on the hottest of days, the pipes were always slightly cool to the touch. After playing hard with friends, one of the great pleasures was to rest one's forehead against the silver. There, with one eye peering straight into the glowing paint, the other on the buildings and trees before me, I tried to bring the two images together and make the city seem afloat on an ocean of silvery waves.

Our modest apartment on the second floor of the building had only one bedroom, which my mother occupied. When I first arrived, I immediately noticed not only the sweet odors emanating from her as in my early childhood but also the caustic smells of her medicines, which sat on the dresser and on the silver tray by her bedside table. Curious mementos filled the apartment, kitsch-like dolls and platters and a large poster celebrating The Song Festivals of Romania with hordes of girls in white peasant blouses bowing to Romanian royalty. These decorations had been the work of my mother's great-aunt Rose (not to be confused with Zalman's wife, Grandma Rose). She had been sent from New York City to Miami Beach to administer the doses and to cook and clean for my invalid mother. Her tyrannical overprotectiveness had caused my mother to beg, in letter after letter to my father, that Aunt Rose be recalled. With my arrival imminent—evidently an enormous rebuff to my aunt's desire to keep my mother insulated from everyone—Aunt Rose packed her bags and in a great huff went back up North.

There was no bedroom for me, and, instead, I was assigned the living room where Aunt Rose had also lived. It was to be where I played and slept, occasionally overturning a chair cushion or pulling a book from a shelf and catching the trapped watery whiff of my great-aunt's cheap perfumes and colognes. A big closet at one end of the room held two pull-down Murphy beds, one for me, and the other for my sister who would arrive later from New York. Pulled down, the bed stuck out into the room like a sickness-whitened tongue.

All the doors in the apartment, including the one leading to the hall, were inset with louvered panels which let air circulate between rooms. To block light or reduce noise, another, smaller door panel set within the door closed over the louvers. At night, I would stand on a chair and peer through the downward slanting slats, watching the feet of people going up and down the hall. People walked by trailing cooking smells or limped past with canes. Mrs. Goldstein, the wife of the building's owner, trod the hall's faded carpets with an imperious stride. Her coming and going made me pull back, but I could hear her loudly talking to herself long after her feet went by.

At the far end of the hall, there was an elevator that my mother used between our second-floor rooms and the lobby and street. But I was always too impatient and took the stairway right outside our door. Midway down the steps, there was a landing with a little window and ledge on which I deposited the potatoes and vegetables from dinner that I didn't want to eat. Often at the table, I sneaked this food, boiling hot from the serving plate, into my pants pocket where it burnt through painfully to my thigh. When I was told the story of the young Spartan boy who hid a fox, nibbling at his ribs, under his cloak, I suddenly felt not only clever but also heroic. Whoever cleaned the halls must have surmised where these little bits of food came from, but my secret was never given away.

The bottom of the stairs led to a rather large lobby sheathed in imitation speckled marble and filled with ornate armchairs and couches swathed in a white cloth flecked with gold thread, a ubiquitous fabric that at times seemed to cover all the interior surfaces of Miami Beach. These bulky, voluminous pieces of furniture, having escaped from nineteenth-century French drawing rooms, tended to engorge the frail nut-brown residents of the Hudson Arms who, flailing arms and legs, could barely sit upright on the billowy mounds of stuffed fabric.

And it was here, in the lobby, and by candlelight, that we held our hurricane parties, singing funny songs and performing skits while heavy gusts made noises in the window seams that sounded like howling cats and off-key orchestras.

For children, the hurricanes were divine provender, a feast of petty adult-rule breaking concerning mealtimes and bedtimes. At all hours of those stormy nights, while wind battered the casement windows and rising waters lapped at the marble entry steps, the halls were filled with running and screaming pajama-clad children. They scurried in and out of apartments where the residents, succumbing to the feverish excitement themselves, fed them outlawed snacks and candies.

And then the grownups, caught in the heightened thrill of the threatening storm, they too started playing practical jokes on each other. My father joined in this general rout of decorum by sitting down at the telephone and dialling up people in the building and exclaiming in thick Yiddish, "Do you know there's a hurricane out there?" He liked this so much that he began dialling numbers randomly, addressing in the same hysterical Yiddish whoever in Dade County picked up the phone. Convulsed in laughter, with tears running down his cheeks, he kept at it until the winds finally brought down the telephone lines.

All this activity only subsided with the storm blowing itself out, usually in a morning of milky light and thick fog. This calm called for excursions outside to the beaches past the automobiles powdered with the ocean's salt and laurelled with fallen twigs and branches. Back from the water, the beach had become a treasure trove of dead fish, sodden household furniture, and the splintery boards of some unlucky boat.

The storms battering the Florida coast sanctioned among the Jewish families of the Hudson Arms a kind of collective hi-jinx, a sort of rewriting of communal helplessness into a celebratory comic fatalism. Another instance of Jewish gallows humor? For I am thinking that the embattled *shtetl* life of the European Jew, its very encirclement by gentile otherness and hostility, also produced an endless—interminable—discursiveness of comic conversation, linguistic and societal in nature but concerned with life and fate. Denied so many other avenues of action, the armies of European Jews marched into battle not on their feet but on their tongues, on words and sentences, on puns, sarcasms, and scatological speech.

In my childhood, the apartment houses of Miami Beach provided a vestigal reenactment of this universe of European Jewish chatter. At the Hudson Arms, this restaging took place beyond the wide doors of the lobby onto the patio, an essential feature of virtually every apartment house in Miami Beach. There was a village quality to these slabs of pink concrete with their white painted outdoor chairs and loungers, their tables and umbrellas. One might have thought of separate apartments, of single individuals in that building until one went out into the patio where the intermingled babble of the residents fused into a single organism, the veins of which flowed together as Yiddish, Russian, German, assorted regionalisms and dialects, and an English so inflected by accents that it sounded like a crowd of people spitting. All spoke at the top of their voice, whispering only when it was necessary to insult someone nearby, a muted sound so irregular in the sluicegate of words that immediately everyone else would fall silent.

This talking began shortly after breakfast, with words still smelling of sweet danish and coffee, and it went late into the night fueled by schmaltz-laden dinners and schnapps. A daily truce stopped the yammering only for midday meals and the afternoon heat when people either took naps in their apartments or walked over to the ocean a few blocks away. It was then that one noticed the chirping of the songbirds that nested in the trees.

At the edge of the patio there grew a tall eucalyptus, the dead man's skin tree as it was called, since its bark, soft to the touch, could be pulled away in papery sheets with the fingernails. This tree has a curiously recurring place in memory, not only for its unforgettable name, which I associate with the muslin wrappings of Egyptian mummies and the cadavers of the movie screens, but because its pale colorings are faintly tinged with red and so resemble my own and my father's skin. Few things disturbed me more than seeing, in my father's nursing home, the scaly, mottled skin of his forearms, like the bark of that tree, sticking out of his hospital gown.

As well, in the nearly Brownian movements of childhood, the tree was something like a tribal locus for the Hudson Arms's small complement of children. Under its branches, we discussed our plans for the day, our complaints against parents and grandparents, and argued over the petty disagreements among ourselves. We stuck messages to each other under slivers of its bark. Where the roots sprang from the ground there was a wide patch of dirt, the only dirt we were allowed to play in, suitable for throwing penknives into or for digging miniature fortifications. And I often found myself, when in distress or hurting from some words of my parents, leaning against it, aimlessly peeling away at the tree trunk.

When the mood took us, we went as a flock of birds over to Washington Avenue, one of Miami Beach's widest streets. It was a main thoroughfare of the area we lived in, South Beach, a part of town noted for the fact that its residents were mainly poor, often elderly retirees from the Jewish ghettos of the North. The avenue was always teeming with activity. Up and down its wide sidewalks marched the elderly, stricken with Old Testament vicissitudes, the foreign tourists seeking color, the children, the shoppers rummaging through the clothes bins and vegetable stands which crowded the sidewalks.

In this neighborhood, one saw nothing of the rich green lawns, the tall straight trunks of Royal palms or the sparkling waters of the bay for which the resort was famous. Here, the open air fruit and vegetable stands were run by Jews from Eastern Europe or the Middle East who hoarsely hawked their goods to anyone passing by. Delis, bakeries, coffee shops comprised a good portion of the street, as though expressing a certain anxiety about food. Between them stood narrow, stiflingly hot clothing stores, their pro-prietors unable to afford the air conditioning which was ubiquitous in the better sections of Miami Beach. It amazed me that these shop owners could sit in those ovens behind the counters or that anyone, once inside, would willingly want to try on a suit or jacket.

On the corner of Fifteenth Place, only a short block south of our street, stood the Cameo Theater, its rotunda faced in pinkish sea coral, a remnant of an earlier elegance to the neighborhood. Its interior resembled something like a cave or a temple where, seated on mildewed velveteen, one watched second-run movies. I had seen only two films in Brooklyn, *The Werewolf* with Lon Chaney Junior and *The Road to Morocco* with Bob Hope, Bing Crosby, and Dorothy Lamour. And so when we first came to Miami Beach, I spent many hours in the air-conditioned Cameo, particu-larly on hot summer afternoons when the admission was only fifteen cents. I would have spent many more except that in 1947, the Cameo began running *The Jolson Story* with Larry Parks, a high point of senti-mental kitsch, which drew the poor residents of South Beach in such returning numbers that it ran for nearly ten years straight. The film's story—Jolson rebels against his father and, instead of studying to be a can-tor, becomes a jazz singer—reminded its audience of theirs and their own children's bitter-sweet apostasies. For myself, the film vaguely replayed the Gideon story of rebellion which I had all but internalized. But the Jolson tale was also a synecdoche, an Ur-tribal meditation on modern Jewry and its fate in an assimilated world, and the adults left the theater with wet eyes, purged as by an Aristotelean catharsis.

At the same time, the movie was surely a spectacle made precisely for a place like Miami Beach; in it, a white actor, Larry Parks, plays a char-acter who half the time appears in minstrel show blackface, appears, half the time, as it were, with makeup around the eyes through which his white skin peeks. There can be no mistake that a white man is playing the role, that the disguise is to be taken literally *as disguise*. As with so many of the other illusionary set-ups of Miami Beach, the film requires there to be some gimmick or sleight of hand by which one's identity in the midst of make-believe can be re-affirmed. In later years, Parks, who entertained at many Miami Beach hotels, was often greeted by local cit-izens as "Mr. Jolson."

Endless days with the thermometer in the eighties and nineties, heat filming everything, compounded into a coat made of irritants and perspiration. But, again, I think of the early mornings, the coolest and quietest part of my days, when a faint mist off the ocean left droplets of water on every leaf and branch, when even the tiny blackish green lizards that normally leapt about the yards were made sluggish by the cold. As though the Beach, transplanted from its languor or from its frenetic resort-life pace, had attained the composed and harmonious calm of an old seaside painting. Such stillnesses, in which everything is serene, held in tensionless relation, comes back to me when I sit at my desk now, paper under hand. I am dreaming of art, of poetry, of that "rested totality" that Louis Zukofsky, one of my mentors in writing, spoke about as the highest achievement of an art form. If the memory goes back, it also flows forward to, and beyond, the present. Almost as though the world, on those peculiar Florida mornings, had achieved the surcease it seems to cry for in moments of horror or destruction.

But I remember too, the war fever, and that during those years of the Forties, the morning silence was short-lived, broken by the U.S. Army marching band which at 7 AM each day drummed its way from the oceanfront hotels where troops on R & R were billeted, to march along Fifteenth Street right under our windows. As it passed the Hudson Arms, I often stood in the entranceway, drawn ambivalently from the morning stillness by the tin glamor of the parade—after all, my own father was an officer of this same army somewhere in the North. The band, playing Sousa marches and the National Anthem, followed the street into Flamingo Park where troops wheeled around the baseball fields in waves of flashing brass and silver. But almost daily, as the hot sun rose and beat down on the formation, great blots of sweat appeared on the shirt fronts and under the arms of the musicians; the music lost its ebullience, the marchers their precision. Confusion stirred among the ranks; soldiers missed the timing of their steps and the rows of men, once straight, became ragged snakelines. Soon, dismissal was sounded, and the men slunk away into the shade of the park dragging their instruments. They would return singly to their hotels, to gather about the pools or sit in the cocktail lounges where, now, only 3.2 beer was served. This near-comical rout without real enemy must have contributed to my later behavior at college where I was one of the few students ever to fail ROTC.

By mid-afternoon, heat wavered off the six-lane-wide expanse of Washington Avenue's asphalt. The sun made the tops of parking meters gleam like the bald heads of bathers standing in some gentle surf. Kress's department store, with its clanking air-conditioning going full blast, swirling together the heady smells of sea-salt, sweat, caramelized popcorn, and burnt coffee, was an oasis amid the heat-baked concrete of the avenue. Here I met my first friends, Alvin, whom I found standing between counters overflowing with button packets and idiotic straw hats, and Amy, whom I sat next to at the Kress's lunch counter where soda phizzed from a chrome spigot.

Amy was all dark and slim like an Indian maiden, her bright white teeth shining out of a tanned face. She wanted to be an actress, she told me, and had only the day before been an extra, playing a Filipino child in the film *They Were Expendable*, a war movie about MacArthur and PT boats that was being made on the little uninhabited islands in Biscayne Bay. As it turned out, Amy lived in my building and we became fast friends and companions.

Alvin reminded one of an overgrown child; he was tall for his age, but with a frame still hung with folds of baby fat. He had the whitest Russian skin, something he inherited from his mother, whose thick Moscow accent and pale handsome face like those found in Russian church icons breathed an otherworldly life into their cramped apartment. Alvin's father, a short jolly man with the physique of a wrestler, was in the rag business. Usually he dressed in workpants and a T-shirt, but once I saw him with a tie around his thick neck, collar open, his bulbous Adam's apple quivering like a rabbit under his coat.

Alvin's family was even more impoverished than my own. It was in Espanola Way, a few blocks south of 15th Street, that Alvin lived, a narrow rundown street and one of the poorest on the Beach. The apartment buildings on the block were arranged Spanish style, in little courts fronting fake fountains and wells. Rainwater had stained the walls, and hand-sized flakes of paint lay close to the buildings. Enormous black palmetto bugs scurried brazenly across the patios over the lips and down into the blackness of the imitation wells where residents often dropped little bits of garbage or half-eaten foodstuffs. As with many places one looked in Miami Beach, one found first chimera, then seediness.

Later, at the corner of Espanola and Drexel, my father went into a bit of a sideline with Bob and Joe, two ex-New York policemen, who opened a detective agency. The down-at-heels atmosphere of the street, with its cheap apartments and flophouse hotels, provided an apt setting. There was, in truth, not much crime in Miami Beach at that period, so the two "detectives" mainly engaged in spying on straying husbands and wives or in preventing the petty thievery in the department stores of nearby Washington Avenue. To give their nearly bogus enterprise some authenticity, they pasted onto the office walls glossy 8 x 10 photographs of heinous crimes and accidents. When I visited with my father, I would gaze at these pictures of bludgeoned corpses, of people with crowbars through their skulls, of cars flipped over in a carnage of heads, arms, and legs.

How my father connected with these two ex-policemen has escaped my memory. Possibly, having once worked with him in New York, they came asking for favors, willing to run errands or distribute advertising literature for him. It may also have been a case of my father, generous to a fault in his impoverishment, imagining himself a man of affairs, lending out money he didn't have and committing himself to favors he couldn't fulfill, especially to his old New York cronies who had trailed South. But a detective agency? My mother was astonished at the unseemliness and missed no opportunity to ridicule the business.

Certainly, the two bumbling ex-cops elicited no confidence as crime solvers. Indeed, there was one long period in which Bob limped around with an ankle-to-thigh cast, having broken his leg in three places while trying to learn jujitsu. Every time my mother laid eyes on him, she'd break into a weepy laughter. And Joe, who had the raspy voice of a *film noir* character, drove an old convertible that was always breaking down. His wife was constantly throwing him out, and so he would come to our house for dinner in an overworn golfing shirt ballooned out by a beer-belly paunch and flecked with cigar ashes.

Central Beach Elementary School was distinguished from South Beach Elementary School by the fact that it drew pupils from both the poorest and wealthiest families on Miami Beach. The one private school, Oxford or Cambridge was its name as I recall, was for misfits, problem children, usually of the wealthy, who'd been such nuisances in the public schools that a paper trail of suspensions and displinary actions led ultimately to its door.

Central Beach, a block-long rambling structure in the Spanish style with pale yellow stuccoed walls and red tile roofs, had a student body that was overwhelming Jewish. The few gentile students, it was joked, met in their respective gender bathrooms on such days as Rosh Hoshanah or Purim. The faculty, a mix of bright young women and spinsterish matrons, was dominated by our principal, Miss D., a tall angular woman who greeted us every morning over the PA system with "The Star Spangled Banner" sung in her own off-key contralto. Despite these regular patriotic morning outbursts, there were rumors that Miss D.'s sympathies lay, darkly, elsewhere. The occasion for such gossip may well have been the May Day celebrations, the school's most elaborate holiday extravaganzas, over which Miss D. presided like an impresario. As I remember, in the yard, each class had its individual maypole. When all the students were assembled and began their dance, each child would be given a colored band to wrap around the class pole. The school yard, with its high posts, flashing ribbons and screaming children, resembled nothing so much as a medieval *kermis*.

Elementary school was by no means the be-all and end-all of our education, for there existed among almost all of the families of my school mates, a subcurrent of assimilationist tendencies. In the nineteen forties, Jews—even if their forebears had resided in America before the Revolutionary War—saw themselves as late arrivers. Thus, almost every public motive or action was marked not only by an obvious sense of civic duty but by a desire to be accepted and to belong. On Miami Beach, proof of one's social belongingness took some bizarre collective forms such as the election, year after year, of gentile councilmen and mayors, evidence of a Jew's Americanized tolerance and, perhaps, fear of other Jews. As well, the tensions of difference threw the more well-off local Jews into exorbitant escapades of cultural philanthropy. From accumulations of often barbaric and unlettered wealth, concert halls and libraries were generously endowed.

But this urge toward refinement, if not for oneself then for one's family members, transcended rich and poor. Among children of my age, the acquisition of Culture with a capital C was the function of after-school afternoons. The darning needles of parvenu strivings embroidered the Beach with little eyelets of dancing schools and conservatories, each catering to a different social class.

My sister Tena and I attended Miss Green's Tap, Dance and Ballet Studio on lower Drexel Avenue, the juxtaposition of the words *tap* and *ballet* sufficient clue to the status of this institution. Miss Green's, housed in an old poorly-lit storefront, damp with the sweat of little bodies and the ever-present humidity, had an inimitable odor of its own, one that seemed to attract a large audience of bugs and spiders which scurried along the walls and ceilings oblivious to the lessons. Miss Green, a wiry woman in her thirties, was, on any one afternoon, a ringmaster to a thunderous inattentive and uncoordinated herd of third and fourth graders. Two fates worse than death awaited anyone taking lessons there. Crushed toes, eyes poked by elbows whirling past one, were as nothing compared with these mortifications. One was to have to dance with girls in the inevitable pairings-up for the ballroom instruction; the other, even worse, occurred when there were not enough girls to make an even match-up, and one had to learn the four-step in the embrace of another school boy. These embraces were centrifugal in nature. They began in mutual antagonism under the watchful eye of Miss Green, shortly to escalate into wild parody as one boy tried to stomp on the other's feet and so sending them both spiralling across the floor to knock down the smaller children who could not get out of the way.

When my mother realized that Miss Green's was hopelessly *déclassé*, she enrolled us in the Miami Beach Conservatory. The Conservatory, a white modern building once housing a number of dentists' offices, was all curves and arches. After Miss Green's I was impressed by the cleanliness of the structure and by the black mahogany piano which sat on a pedestal, the perfect altar on which to sacrifice a child's afternoon. Dance lessons were now a thing of the past, and we graduated to elocution and drama under the auspices of Miss M., who looked like a cross between Clara Bow and Jane Wyman. Miss M. taught us pronunciation and drama, and when she enunciated words such as *polite* or *courtesy* (or was it *curtsy?*) they produced a wide bulging of her exophthalmic eyes. But Miss M.'s flawless diction was not only an example for us; it was also a linguistic restraining net thrown over her own well-hidden Southern drawl, which peeped like an ugly bird through the diction in lightning flashes of anger or frustration. When she became irritated and let her tongue slip into the lower orders of speech, into an intemperate widening of her jaws, the decorous building blocks of well-said syllables crumbled before our eyes and ears. Wasn't this actually the lesson, this matter of disguises, I think we must have thought, as Miss M., fluttering her eyelids and exaggerating the movements of her jaw, battered at the *deses*, *dems*, and *doses* of our New York accents?

During our recesses, we would walk out of the back doors of the Conservatory and play under the massive pines and cascading Spanish mosses that grew along the banks of one of Miami Beach's canals. Into its waters, we tossed the fallen pine cones, watching them float past, moving on under little concrete bridges while we silently mouthed our new pronunciations, as though we had cast away the old rotten husks of syllables we had learned somewhere else.

Where did reality-culture live in that absurd agglomeration of the meretricious and the patently false which constituted the foundations of the life in Miami Beach? Curiously, I found a consuming sense of something real in books, not because they were any less false or mediocre than the life outside them (my school textbooks or the ones found in the children's section of the library were as deceitful as any), but because they exhibited a coherence the world around me did not have. The book was dependable, its characters, well, they acted "in character"; the places in which they lived or where they walked and talked, they too had a logical consistency in marked contrast to the concrete dreamscapes and fabled facades of this resort town. As a young person, then, it was only a matter of deciding which part of the world to believe in, the one around me or the one in the text, with its rules of syntax and grammar.

Thus, it was no accident that Book Day was my favorite assembly program of the year. Such emphasis on story books and history made of the school a genuine anomaly in the spa-like atmosphere of the city. Its annual parade of pupils, each dressed up as a character from a book, giving little speeches as they marched across the stage, were very much my version of the shadows thrown on the wall in Plato's Parable of the Cave. In my fifth grade year, I entered the Book Parade contest dressed as Long John Silver from Stevenson's *Treasure Island*. The clothes I wore came mainly from my mother's closet, her long baggy pants, a flouncy white blouse, a great wide black belt with a conspicuous gold buckle, a Spanish torero type of hat with a flat crown. My crutch consisted of one leg of the easel I painted on. But I could not find any way of affixing a peg leg to this outfit, and this problem led me to write one of my first poems, one that I spent hours composing and memorizing.

I, MICHAEL, aged eight, reading. "It was no accident,
then, that Book Day was my favorite . . ."

For the Parade, I remember tying my lower leg back to my thigh,
neatly disguised in my mother's baggy trousers and hobbling with the
crutch across the stage. When I came to the middle, I whirled and faced
the audience. "I am Long John Silver," I shouted, "and I make people

shiver./And when I find who stole my peg leg,/I'll cut out his *l-i-v-e-r!*"
My performance drew enormous applause and at the end of the assembly,
I was told that I had won one of the prizes, a copy of *Tom Sawyer*. At
home, I carefully examined the book. It was an Alfred A. Knopf edition,
a Borzoi book with thick creamy pages and a beautiful, lightly tinted cover.
On the spine, the Borzoi dog in a fine lined drawing, seemed oblivious to
the world beyond the pages.

For me, then, the crudeness and vulgarity of Miami Beach's resort life
was held at bay by walls of printed words. At the public library adjacent to
the museum, I checked out three or four books a week, from "boys'" fiction
by writers such as Howard Pyle or Albert Payson Terhune, to works on science or science fiction including the books of such varied authors as Jules
Verne, Arthur C. Clarke, and Robert Heinlein. For a time, I seemed to live
in particular in Verne's tales, narratives that came enclosed in handsome
illustrated editions with explorers and scientists dressed like European gentlemen, its military officers wearing the red tunics of the Hussars. The
machinery, the most wonderful aspect of all, from moon rockets to steam-
driven mechanical elephants, contained internal compartments furnished
with overstuffed sofas and chairs reminiscent of Victorian living rooms.

Because I had fair skin and burnt easily, I often read in the afternoons,
waiting for the sun to set sufficiently for me to take a swim at the beach
or pool. Even then, there was a reluctance on my part to rise and go play
with my friends.

For it was not only an isolating time in reading, which gave me a sense
of being apart, but I was also accumulating a hoard of scientific terms,
words I looked up in the dictionary but could barely pronounce. I had
acquired a kind of tongue-tied second language, one I couldn't share with
friends owing to their lack of interest or because of my fears about pronunciation already existing from my speech-impeded days in New York. It
was this other, nearly secret language, which opened onto depths and vistas of wonderment, that I loved most. How talk—and in what funny
sounding way—about the mysteries of the skies or about the magical qualities of measure and number? Possibly I came to study and to write poetry
in the belief that these bifurcated streams of language could be united,
united in either the silence of a book-lined room or the hushed atmosphere of a laboratory, places where one didn't have to speak.

If one had the capability of making a record of all the occasions of one's encounters with language, I imagine that such a listing would approximate all the moments one had been alive and either awake or dreaming, an unrealized simultaneity between what we think and what we have lived. Marcel Proust came near to achieving a simulacrum of such a record, we recall, not by any conscious will to remember everything, but by an open receptivity, an effacement before the mind's capacity to intuit and recollect. The bones or struts of the record, which are syntax (Nietzsche famously remarked of the organizing power of language that "if God is dead, how come we still have grammar?"), truly undergird any sense of substantiality or integrity to a life. Yet even as language "makes" something, thus propelling us toward an edifice of event or place, it also induces glimmer, nuance, hint. We always overwrite, add more than we meant.

I am reminded of a picture from the Bialystok book given to me by David Sohn which provokes a conflicted reverie bordering on obsession. The picture shows a grey-bearded man in *shul*, his body wrapped like a bulky earth-borne cloud in a spotless white prayer shawl and yarmulka. Its caption reads, *"An aged man learning."* The photograph gives off psychic emanations as though it were an ink blot or Tarot card, a fragment of Jewish High Arcana which darkens my experience of reading as it radiates with an ambivalent mixture of piety and uselessness. There is no question that the social history of the Jew, especially for antisemites, is bound to such a figure. To the Jew as practitioner of occult ritual, to the Jew's seeming preference for the inward modes of contemplation as opposed to the outward cult of action. For what is depicted here is the mind's enclosure in the otherworldly, in the alien. In that, the picture joins with images of Proust's cork-lined room and with the secret recesses of the Rothschilds' counting house where the calculus of bank stocks and arbitrage are read, according to those who, in their hatred of Jews, venerate the *Protocols of the Elders of Zion*, as a kind of Torah. Inflaming images to the masses of working men, to laborers. . . .

But then there is this other level of the experience of holding a book in one's hand, plunging me back into my childhood. In a swoon of similitude, this very same picture opens up onto sheltered harbors, onto miniscule and, in a way, inhibited vistas of quiet and charm, of remembering how I nestled myself on the old fat striped couch in our sunken Brooklyn living room where I first began my reading while out of the corner of my eye I could see the wheels of cars and wagons rumble past the windows. The child's mind flickers, goes like a bird between the book and the street. As I think of it, the street represented all sorts of fascinated dangers and entanglements, especially the world outside convulsed by the Second World War. A whole generation of readers have been marked in this way.

It may be that the inner etiology of the *dovener*, of the ritual reader—and what reading does not invoke a ritual?—comes as a force, one that rushes from inside to the surface of the skin in order to meet one's enemies in the world. Surely part of my arrogance and shyness lies there at that margin.

As well, the absorbing enthrallment in story worked throughout my childhood as an abeyance, a calming of—in my case—the nervousness and anxiety generated by fears for my mother's health. Here, to read was to be passively protective, to be mouse-like, to upset no one by noise or clumsy activity. Best that I not ask her to play with or entertain me, but to curl myself away with a book and do no harm. Later, in Florida, the prolonged absences of my father as he settled his affairs in New York figured into this equation, so that reading was equally a self-disappearance, a flight from integuments and contingencies not of my making.

And because of these tensions, now there was an open floodgate to reading's romanticisms: for such too were the shaded days in the hammock at Peekskill, New York, where we often spent summers, insects buzzing and dark and light playing over the open pages of a book, a romance of youth whose idleness is all preludium to beauty, to bodies in embrace. To the depths of sexuality which the mind dreaming across the page created. Was it an illustrated edition of *The Swiss Family Robinson* or some other tale of families shipwrecked or castaways which I pored over in the August heat of upstate New York? Parts of my being were formed around those lightly tinted engravings where young girls, sylph-like, emerged from tropical lagoons or forested swimming holes to lie sunning on grassy outcroppings of rock. All those were but romantic collocations, the way the child of a middling bourgeois family might both meet and avoid the extremities of life.

Much later, however, after college, I was to find myself bathed in my own sweat in the stifling retreat of my Aunt Jen's attic, surrounded by her Classics and yet shut away from the shriekings of her voice and of the TV.

The two sounds were chopped together into odd synchronicities of madness. By that time, the picking up of a book was another, related form of mind-protection, an armoring made of words. If the book happened to enrapture, all to the good, but, at that time in my beginning adulthood, even the hard bite of dry knowledge chained one, like Ulysses, to a post, resisting the call of disturbing siren voices.

In my feeling for certain sound-banished precincts, in my need for book-filled allurements of quiet and solitude, there was always also intermingled the desire for narrative, for the way silence encloses those constructs made of beginnings and endings, for shaped language which by magic conspired to produce an entity, rounding it off and giving it closure. Or perhaps enclosure, as when a book is suddenly a skein of chain mail, a scaled vest or the iron mask of a swordsman. A story not as mere chatter but as an arc or curve bending finally in on itself, leading one back to silence by resembling in appearance and effect the solidity of a single word. Uttered and gone.

It was this kind of "word," a story or a poem, that flared up as some registration of the world's flux and so was less the speech work of an individual, it seemed to me, than that of a divinity who moment by moment granted meaning to the universe. Meaning was hidden everywhere *in situ*, but always to be granted as revelation to the reader, extricated from some intractable otherness, call it God or Cosmos. I associate the loneliness induced by the reading of serious writing, by the dark nexuses of thought, to come from such an encounter. The poet Paul Celan specifically identified this feeling as a kind of "Jewish loneliness," one borne into the reader's psyche by a word or poem, but also by the special relationship that Jewish culture had to texts and textuality and to the catastrophic sense of history that Jews brought to their reading.

To make shape, to make shapely, to have a "fine hand," to be "well-spoken" both in voice and on the page, suggests a social obligation, that there is, from elsewhere, inside or out, some sort of pressure operating against shape or form and that character is the creative resistance to this pressure. The historical Jew, especially the one, as Sander Gilman reminds us, who figures like some sort of bogeyman in nineteenth-century English literature, is marked by how his language has fallen away from Oxbridge accents and speech rhythms, the Anglo-American model of well-spokenness. The Victorian explanation of the Jew was a racial one of grasping mercantile genes and deformed inwardness, which tied the Jewish tongue into comic-sounding knots.

Yet for the memorialist, a force field surrounds the minutiae of daily life, emanating from even the most unreflected thought process or problem solving, the instrumentalized linguistics of one's existence. This subconscious gossip of language, like the mementoes of a scrapbook, form an aura at once familiar and estranged. And that aura creates moments where we are suddenly challenged by language to bend it to a form, to make it yield like a gesture or action until it becomes an object, separate from us and with a life of its own. And this is not only true for the literary person. The poet Geoffrey Hill refers to the impediments of voicing as "contexture," suggesting that every poetic utterance occurs in "the enemy's country," and that a "poet's words or rhythms are not his utterance so much as his resistance," his unwillingness to follow speech's or silence's easiest line of travel. The exiled poet and the exiled Jew meet for me in this near-blockage of the speech act.

For the child that I was, this demand to speak well was palpable, yet it was accompanied by a nervousness and fear of a stutter or mangled expression, of a verbal gesture or a miswritten word that might evoke adult disapproval. Somewhere, in every childhood, most powerfully where the self is undergoing change or growth, language becomes tinged with fear, almost as though words had sprouted thorns that threaten to stick in one's tongue. That "region of hysteria," as Barthes called our entanglements of language, coupled with an almost infantile desire, was circumscribed for me in the communicative act itself. For a realm existed of words that were perfectly, clearly utterable. But through fear or shame, words would acquire their own life in my mouth, curling over or under themselves, flailing or twisting in the oral cavity until they no longer resembled those thought-sounds held in the mind-box. I cannot think of these anxieties and mortifications, these haltings and accompanying blushes, without also remembering the soothing presence of my mother, the patience and kindness on her face as she guided me through my difficulties.

Also, too, there is an erotics to being tongue-tied or stammering, one which I felt, again in infantile fashion, in my encounters with Miss Zaiderman, my fourth grade teacher, with whom I fell into a kind of dizzying, panicky love. Like my mother, she was kind and gentle and worked many hours after school with my speech problem. Miss Zaiderman was quite tall, with severe but beautiful features; she looked something like a model or one of those heroines in my favorite comic strip, *Prince Valiant*. She could easily have been an actress, but one who took only intellectually demanding parts, a Vanessa Redgrave or Katherine Hepburn. Under the severity, there was an affecting warmth which flooded her face when she stood in front of the class with her square, mannish shoulders and long brown hair slightly streaked with gray. She was quite friendly with the students and occasionally after class invited them to her apartment, which was not very far from where I lived.

Being in Miss Zaiderman's presence upset me in ways I couldn't comprehend. I was embarrassed at my own feelings, of course, never mentioning them to anyone. And yet the one thing I desired more than anything else was to be invited to her after-school gatherings. These were, on the face of it, rather harmless affairs: a matter of milk and cookies, and while nibbling away on these things, discussions about geography or literature. And yet, from the first, when my mother asked where I had been in the afternoon as I straggled into the house just before dinner, I would mumble something about playing late with my friends. Since I had not missed dinner with the family, one of the cardinal rules of our home life, not much was made of my lateness.

One time, however, Miss Zaiderman invited three or four of us to come the following day to her house for dinner. What should I do, I asked myself? I could not bring myself to tell my mother or ask for permission. So the next evening, when I arrived home at eight o'clock at night, long after dinner had concluded, to find a worried face on my mother, I concocted an elaborate story of how I had fallen in the playground and bumped my head, and how for an hour or two forgot who I was, wandering around the streets of Miami Beach until my head cleared and then came home. My mother looked rather skeptically at me while I recited this absurd story, but she said nothing. Nor did she grasp me and look at my supposedly injured head. The outrageousness of my excuse seemed to put her in a thoughtful mood. For even as I had spoken to her, I could sense a darkness across my face which must be telltale visible.

Lying—which I distinguish from not telling, not uttering a held thought—had an almost physiological effect on me and so did not come easy. But my mother went about her business of cleaning and putting away the dishes. The guilt-filled silence that ensued, the space and clearing of a falsehood, was like a place into which the world must collapse. It felt heavy on me, to be there in that quiet kitchen with my mother's back to me. And lying in my bed that night, I experienced a tremendous urge to say something, to disburden so as to right the event and put my life back in balance.

In my mind, I relate my feeling toward language and poetry to events like this, events in which one experiences the whole inarticulateness of one's physical and historical person, the very heaviness of the body, as only something pressing to be a word, as though a word or sound were an extrusion of the pressures upon the body. These pressures implied an ethics of words— and later, one of poetry. Given this feeling, the false word, the word struck loose from its possible home in the world, from its contact with truth and reality even in the name of art, would exhibit an otherworldly purity. Many poets, I know, have sought such a word liberated from contingency. The poetry of such purity, the words of *l'art pour l'art*, have often dazzled me but left me bereft of my world. In my own practice of writing, I have come to a word or a phrase and, finally, a poem by a kind of stumbling in language, a letting of words and listenings grow in me until, when I cast them forth, I could hear something of my need or desire in the structure of the language.

I understood too that such a structure, which arrived for me with an almost animal bluntness, could only be truth and not Truth. Always partial, no poem contains all of poetry even as, in the moment of reception, it threatens to be so. For the words of others that have moved me most are overwhelming feral presences, wild and combative, fighting to possess me.

And now that I reflect back, it seems that the mystery of our singular desires, of wanting *this* and not *that*, such as in a youthful infatuation or romance, also has something of this combative architecture. At least this was the case with my "love" of Miss Zaiderman, a lesson for me of how love or desire can separate one out.

My first intimation of nearly adolescent sexual feelings began I think with Amy, that is, unless one counts the cloudy remembrance (possibly invented) I have of approaching my mother's breast as an infant, her black hair spilling down her shoulder, the aureole of the nipple a little low and to the right, the flesh soft and yielding looming before me, the cloying intermingled aromas of perspiration, milk, and perfume.

I was ten years old. Amy lived down the hall with her divorced mother, Anna, a dark-haired, swarthy-skinned woman who had been further tanned to a gypsy brown by the Florida sun. Anna was active, intense, a study in constant decisiveness and quick movement. In the nearly black skin of her face, her large, goggled eyes swam excitedly, darting this way and that over the world. Between her secretarial jobs and her fierce and abandoned dating in the evenings, she flitted briefly through the family apartment in tight pastel summer dresses like an exotic insect.

Also living with the mother and daughter was Amy's grandmother, a white-haired woman named Sophie who, in appearance and demeanor, resembled one of those puritanical elders of Norman Rockwell's illustrations. In the apartment, she stood apart, frail but upright in a shapeless paisley dress, her skin, as though a critique of her daughter's physical sensuality, covered by a pale powdery down which the sunlight set aglow.

Amy was a bit of a tomboy and liked playing with me. But what definitively threw us together during those years when my father was still living mainly in New York was our mothers' friendship, both women living their daily lives without the close proximity of men. The two of us were playmates, taken to the beach every day by our mothers or running around in the lobby or playing in the patio or in the living rooms of each other's apartments. Black-haired and dark-skinned like her mother, Amy looked almost part Indian as she jumped from one couch to another or played giddy-yap on the silver painted gas pipes.

As I played with Amy, her flashing bare legs and laughing face brought something secretive and erotic to our games and make-believe. It was as though, for no reason that I could discern, a bifurcation was taking place, that in my enjoyment and activity, two parallel things were going on at once. One—and growing weaker as things developed—was my absorption in what we were doing, a lostness that had once been complete but was now, for the first time, beginning to develop a contour, an edge that another part of me could sense. I was being pulled away from, was being— in the vaguest way—nagged by another impulse which made me look out of myself at Amy, at her long and beautiful body, and feel in myself a desire to touch or grasp her. When, for instance, we wrestled, as we often did, my desire was not to best her, to pin her on the grass but, win or lose, to have as much of her body as possible press against me. Even the thought of this, before play began, was enough to arouse me.

This duality in our game playing crystallized and became absolutely clear to me in its two extravagant parts one hot day, when even the louvered doors of the apartments in the Hudson Arms were left open to catch a bit of cross ventilation and I, as I often did, wandered into Amy's apartment unannounced. Amy was being fitted by her grandmother for a skirt, and was standing on a kitchen chair in her little white tennis shoes and panties. My eyes went immediately to Amy's chest where slight curves of flesh were already beginning to force her nipples forward. Amy waved unembarrassed to me from the chair, but the grandmother who had not seen me come in, whirled around to look angrily at me, then grabbed Amy's shirt and threw it over the front of her.

I think back: wasn't this gesture the first furtive drawing of a curtain across the whole area of sex, furtive not because it attempted to cover but to uncover as well? Under the thin cloth of Amy's shirt the outlines of her breasts were plainly visible. The gesture had merely translated them into another realm, no longer as parts of her body, but figurations of some symbolic order which dwelt not in her but in me. For they began to reappear in my daydreams and in my thoughts at night just before falling asleep. And it was not long before other disembodied parts, legs and necklines and the secret interiors between a woman's thighs, joined this order.

Nor were parts of men's bodies excluded, for there was Joey D., a slightly older boy, who, because he was older and stronger, was something of a leader. Joey, one night, under the stands of the Flamingo Park baseball field, initiated a half-dozen of us into the circle jerk. Joey was a Catholic, one of the few who went to Central Beach Elementary school, and not only was his uncircumcised penis different looking, but the fact that he was a gentile gave a deeply secretive air to the occasion. Now too the male sexual organ entered the alienated zone of the erotic.

Thus, this curtain drawn across what was forbidden to see, though of course everything forbidden had been seen, was also like a surgical instrument; it excised parts of a body and gave them a new life of their own in one's mental life. The furtiveness disturbed me; at an early age I was suddenly a moralist, and I remember many times flying into a fury when my friends around me were using four-letter words.

In all these early and now remote erotic promptings, what is clear is how doubled such feelings were, simultaneously joining and separating one with the desired person or object. Such doubling is part of writing as well. A word is taken up by a writer both as a means of reaching toward something and as a way of differentiating it from mere sound or noise, which means, as with desire, it seeks to include and exclude. The syntax of language and the syntax of eroticism meet each other in a poet's fetishistic relationship to a word or name. In this, the body parts of articulated speech resemble the constellated limbs of the one who is desired.

As I've been writing this, I've felt the need to insert a sort of apologia, to give some substance to my indulgence.

Thinking the past and putting it in words, the memorialist often tries to enter the nostalgia of a former time or the sweet comfortableness of his or her processes of thought. Self-satisfying gestures. Is there another way? I am reading from Joseph Roth's *Job*: "many years ago there lived in Zucknow in Russia, a man named Mendel Singer." A curious process leads me from my chair to Zuchnow, and in the process of reading not even one whole sentence passes before I have lost my life and am living Mendel Singer's. To read is to enter; to write is to isolate.

This is also the rule of memoir. Jean Starobinski, commenting on Rousseau's *Confessions*, asserts: "The proper place of the inner life is defined solely by the failure to establish any satisfactory relationship with external reality." The endless assays of the past, which constitute the stuff of memoir, are only tangentially related to a conception of time. Words in literary form are always depicting a desired ideality and not the real. And because writing, even at its most spontaneous, is never *now*, it can powerfully reconfigure time and memories. Writing, in effect, creates a rebus of hope. The grammar of reality has given sway to an "as-if" or imaginative grammar of interiority.

What of this interiority? Mandelstam, in his great poetic memoir, *The Noise of Time*, declares that "my memory is inimical to all that is personal." Yet his memoir is one of the most personal documents of twentieth-century Russian literature, charged to the utmost in every sentence and paragraph with detail, observation, character sketch, and personal impression. A case could be made that *The Noise of Time* is a political work, that the immensity of its personal and idiosyncratic reflections constitutes, for Mandelstam, an oppositional response to an ominous collectivity of thought and statism looming on the nearby horizon. Another perspective might suggest that the great density of personal reflection in Mandelstam so objectifies memory that it is cleansed of mere privacy, that it is the clarification of a time, a strong response to a family and an age, as he puts it, that "was tongue-tied from birth."

If one looks back, surely time is rendered as a series of failures to be unravelled, as moments when our energy or our attentiveness was not sufficiently at home to the world's solicitations. We must remember and re-imagine to give our experience its proper depth. Our re-imagining is why writing always seems charged with a kind of buoyancy and even optimism close to hope.

It is not that we do not live our lives; rather, what I have come to feel is that writing is merely another life, dreamlike and tangential to our wakefulness. Its discoveries, while they cannot bridge or bring us into some totality or spontaneous form of life, can add or show us each moment's plenitude. Thus, a writing such as this might not be at all about my life in time but an intervention across time that grants to consciousness a depth of field, a *res potentia* that can weaken or deconstruct self-imposed limitations. The ethics of such a writing would not consist in the programmed logic of its words but in the vocabulary of promised possibilities.

Hence the dissonances of countermemory, those irruptions of remembered scraps or stories that occur disjunctively and outside the smooth flow of narrative time. The Freudian slips or Proustian *madeleines* of our involuntary memory constitute the dialogue of inner life not with the past but with the present.

Here, in the memoir, one's "failure" propels toward the future, toward amends, but in a blind, stumbling way. For the "story" of a writing might be that while the writer is trying to recapture a sociohistorical context to his life or trying to argue with adversaries about the meanings and interpretations of an event, his prose is directed at the unconditioned, the place (perhaps before event) where one's life or one's poems begin. The potential embodied in a piece of writing might consist, then, not in achieving the perfections inherent in a gesture's forms (such as a novel or poem) but in realizing a certain personal rather than linear perfection, a spiritual economy that no form can dictate *a priori*. Such a work might very well be discontinuous and conflate or reorder time because it is meant to be read against the lulling commonalities of form.

Zalman Heller. Grandfather. One Passover season, when he was in his eighties, he was brought by his daughter, my Aunt Ina, and Sid, her husband, to Miami Beach where my family had been living for some years. At that time, before the days of Castro and the Cuban Revolution, the southern end of Miami Beach, was as much an enclave of Judaism as a suburb of Tel Aviv or Williamsburg, Brooklyn. On one five-block stretch of Washington Avenue, the wide north-south main thoroughfare, there were seven synagogues of varying sizes enfiladed between department stores and open-air fruit markets, delis, and small clothing shops. A number of these were capped with gold painted domes; others, with their stained-glass windows and buttressed arches looked vaguely Romanesque as though ready to be disguised as Christian buildings if the need arose. The crowds going to and fro on the streets, colorfully dressed in flowing resort clothing and a wide variety of hats, could easily have passed for the swirling nomadic tribes of the Middle East. At times, in the high winter season, the boulevard looked like an oriental bazaar fashioned by Hollywood's Central Casting.

My grandfather, with Ina and Sid, took rooms in one of the South Beach "kosher" hotels which fronted the ocean, where dietary laws were observed and elevators were put on automatic for the Sabbath hours so that, as their advertisements put it, "no one should be required to operate machinery." My father, because of his public relations business, had professional accounts with a number of these places. And we, as a family, occasionally dined at one where the salt-tinged air intermingled with the faint smoke of burning candles and the rich sounds of Yiddish were counterpointed by the muffled beating of the surf. Even the white of the table-cloths seemed infused with the iridescence of the ocean glimpsed under moonlight through the large plate glass windows.

My grandfather, already touched by senility, had a detached air about him. His pointed beard seemed to twitch every which way as he looked around at the unfamiliar sight of palm trees and deep blue skies and the

MY GRANDFATHER and I, Lummus Park, Miami Beach, 1944. "My grandfather, already touched by senility, had a detached air about him."

coral chain of hotels that ran for miles along the oceanside. He wore a shiny grey suit, white shirt open at the collar, under which one could see a yellowish undershirt and grey sprouting hairs. My aunt had bought him a broadbrimmed panama, the kind a South American gentleman might wear, and this gave the upper half of my grandfather's figure a rakish look somewhat discordant with the thickish European gleam of his pants and heavy polished black shoes.

My grandfather's failing mental powers cast an almost saintly character on his actions. Time and illness had beaten the rigidity out of him. Once a fiery martinet whose sternness had driven my father from his house, he was now like a piece of metal so hammered by the mallet that it received blows unquestioningly and could be pressed into almost any shape prepared for it.

Here on Miami Beach, his habit was to wake early and leave the hotel, aimlessly wandering the palm-lined streets, the grassy parks where he plucked hibiscus blossoms off the bushes. Often he was found sitting on the sands watching the bathers, speaking Yiddish in friendly tones to uncomprehending children who slouched around him in wet, sand-caked bathing suits unsure whether to venerate or laugh at this bemused Reb. Once, miraculously, he arrived at our apartment, drenched in sweat and nearly incoherent, thinking he was back in New York and wanting to "go sit in the backyard," his favorite part of our old house in Brooklyn.

The night of the first *seder* we all gathered at the hotel where the meal and service were to be conducted by a well-known local rabbi, one of my father's close friends in the community. The rabbi's table was placed on a dais above the rest of the diners, and beside the table was a small podium on which rested a *Haggadah* and some ritual objects. The diners were seated at circular tables where, in the center of each, stood the symbolic Cup of Elijah, a glass full to the brim with red wine, at which the knives and forks on the circumference pointed.

When my grandfather appeared with Ina and Sid, he struck me as unusually agitated. This was the first *seder* in many years at which he was not presiding, and this fact must have pierced through his bewilderment, forcing him to acknowledge that age had brought not only a certain abstractedness to his life but loss of control. Formerly, his devoutness had issued forth from him like a mandate to others. His genuine spirituality, principled and harsh in my father's youth, had once projected his presence onto others with inevitable and unquestioned physicality. As a teacher of Hebrew, he had imperially commanded his class, and it was with a teacherly presence, which the Passover liturgy requires, that he had exercised his writ over the ritual table. In his present diminished circumstances, these temporal powers by which he held sway over others had left him.

Perhaps he was privately enraged at his own aging, that his God, He-who-is-Blessed, had humbled him and denied him the role of being His instrument. So it was that as the rabbi on the podium began to chant, my grandfather suddenly rose from his chair. "The wrong place!" he shouted in Yiddish, "Beginning in the wrong place!" The room fell silent, and all eyes turned toward our table as Ina tried to pull him down into his seat. The rabbi on the podium looked to my father, his expression a mixture of both sympathy and annoyance. "Poppa," my father said, as sadly as I've heard him say anything, "Please, poppa." His father sat down, but not to be quiet. As the ceremony started up again, my grandfather began to recite, from memory, and in a voice that could be heard at least a few tables away, his own service of the ritual, picking up the various foods and objects in accordance with his own voice, passing the boiled eggs and the bitter herbs to us on his own timetable. I was hearing again the religious droning of my childhood, and as I looked around, I saw that we were all being carried back to earlier years, making the gestures and the eating of that night merely a whirl of spectres and presences. My father, like a loyal son, was humming along, accompanying my grandfather; we were, one and all, family and relatives, attending to my grandfather's *seder*.

My mother wore a string of amber beads. Where the beads had been drilled, there were faint dark miniscule lines. When the necklace was held up to the light, it was the dark threads, bead to bead, that seemed to form a continuity, to hold them linked together, rather than the white cord on which they were strung. When she died, and I, my sister, and my brother divided up her little bit of jewelry among ourselves, this piece fell to me, and I gave it to my wife.

CONSTELLATIONS OF WAKING

on the suicide of Walter Benjamin
at the Franco-Spanish border, 1940

Something you wrote:
"Eternity is far more
the rustle of a dress

than an idea."
What odd sounds
to listen to
beneath occluded skies
that darken rivers,
Dnieper, Havel, Ebro,

murmuring contained
between
their tree-lined banks . . .

"In the fields
with which we are concerned,

knowledge comes only
in flashes. The text
is thunder rolling

long afterwards."
And thus, and thus . . .

*

These constellations,
which are not composed of stars
but the curls of shrivelled leaves

by which the tree expressed
the notion of the storm. You
lived in storm, your outer life:

"adversities on all sides
which sometimes came
as wolves." Your father—

Europe was your father
who cast you on the path,
hungry, into constellated cities:

Berlin, Moscow, Paris.
Where would
Minerva's owl alight,

on what dark branch
to display its polished
talons?

*

1940
and in Paris, the library
is lost.

Books
no longer on the shelves—
how sweetly

they were "touched," you wrote
"by the mild boredom
of order."

*

Curled leaf,
one among many
on trees that lead

to a border crossing.
But black wolves in France,
they have changed the idea

of eternity. Toward
Port Bou, bright dust
mixing

with the ocean's salt air.
Wave-fleck from train:
each spun light

must have its meaning.
So to consider
as ultimate work

that sea bed of
all citation—
you'd allow nothing of your own—

thus the perfected volume.
No author?
And then no death?

The sea is inscribed
with *The Prayer
for the Dead.* No

author and then
no death? But the leaf
acquired shadow by

the ideal of light,
scattered light
the father

never recognizes.
The books are not
on shelves,

for that was Paris.
This the closed road
from Port Bou

which glistens with the dew
of morning. Redemptive
time

which crystallizes
as tree, as leaf
on the way to a border.

Note to Constellations of Waking:

An homage to Walter Benjamin whose thought flutters inextricably through my own work. His crypto-kabbalism, his relation to Gershom Scholem, his penetrating thoughts on language and his profound worrying of the secular/theological problematic represent the authentic juncture of diasporic thought. It is no accident, given the pressures he embodied in his thinking, that for him the ideal text was one constructed solely of citations from other writers. Hence my own funereal verses on his last days, in particular his late notion on the externality of knowledge and the allegorical nature of all text and history. The contemporary notion of the disappearance of the author which he anticipated in word and deed, culminating in death by his own hand as he sought to escape the Nazis, would seem to provide the Jewish-born (as opposed to the Israeli-born) writer with an exemplary if cautionary tale.

This, from the *Zohar*: "Woe to the generation lacking in shepherds, when the sheep stray, knowing no direction."

I started to write poetry in my late twenties. As with much that had preceded in my life, I blundered into poetry, being previously neither a lover of poems nor aware of their transformative power. As I came toward poetic and personal awareness of my Jewishness, paradoxically through my own deepening sense of secularization and then by way of my turning to poetry and philosophy, it was a few articulations *as poems* that kept faith with the sea changes of my life. Scraps of poetry, like philosophical maxims, became my shepherds, my word paths for entering what seemed to be a latent version of myself. One saw the word, words, as having a twofold power, first to draw one's attention, to cause one to be at an instantaneous remove from the actual dailiness of an activity (this has always been, for me, the subtlest yet least examined meaning of the Book), and, second, to be a haunting. In this latter case, the ghostly powers of words resided, incarnating themselves in one until they were no longer capable of being recognized as mere objects of attention. Via the poem, words were physically incantatory, orders of possession, dilators of consciousness and its apprehensions. Language could be a thrall, a moral animator—this was power and danger—in the life of one who took words in, of one who was a reader. To reformulate Eliot's famous comment in "Tradition and the Individual Talent," the dead poets are not only "that which we know," but "that which we desire." In this sense, any powerful mastery of language occurred under the signs of or even within the strictures of another's poetry, rather than within the free play of language.

In a sense, to be a supplicant before words, before combinations of words, was to gather two intimacies at once, that of the very things words named, the trees, the rocks, the persons and images, etc. and that of a *renaming*: that construct of the poem which collocated all these names of things and yet held them in some new order and relationship and so constituted a new name. Here, in renaming, tradition and freedom coexisted side by side, forming a continuous juncture, which ran directly through the poet. It was this juncture which I felt to be my rootedness in Jewish tradition, and like the living root of a plant that one unearths from the soil to examine closely, there were areas where the cellular structures of the root exchange minerals and nutrients and water with the earth, a boundary membrane where what is dead and what is alive are indistinguishable.

V

Coda/Collage

SUMMER, 1945. My father rented us an old stone house in Peekskill, N.Y. The war was nearly over, the training duties of the National Guard had been phased out, and so on Friday nights, with the sun still high, he would arrive from his New York office still wearing his tie and jacket.

Urbanity, a city-sense, an aura of brownstones and shaded parks, of wrought iron and pavement, of business complex enough to require intelligence but still worthy of being sentimentalized as in a Thirties movie, as banter, as conversation over lunch or in tap rooms. These my father carried with him where ever he went. Even into green countryside of upstate New York. Emerging from his Olds, with packages and little gifts, he cut a figure both dazzling and anachronistic.

My mother would have put on her best housedress, and with fresh makeup, awaited my father on one of the wooden recliners on the front entranceway. The entranceway had a formal cast, two white Greek-like pillars made of wood which held a halfmoon of a shelter over the front door to the house, so that there was the vaguest suggestion of an antebellum mansion. All these memories which must be read through layer upon layer of image and culture.

We also had roles to play. We had minnows to show him when he appeared! My sister and I netted them out of the stream behind the house, put them in a big mason jar which we placed on the fireplace mantle in the living room. The minnows looked like long pencil-thin shards of silver which, as they executed a brilliant eye-catching turn, seemed, for a moment, to reflect back all the light in the room. I watched them for hours. Sometimes I'd forget to pour them back into the stream and find them floating, dull and belly up, in the jar the next morning.

Leaves of a book, each page a moment's home, until a book or chapter closes. Lift your eyes up from a book: you are exiled and yet you are at home. That power.

It was my mother's voice, hysterical for the first time over the phone, calling me. A thread of terror ran through her voice like a streak of grease across a mirror. My father was again quite ill, could I come down to Miami, to the Beach and help her with him? And it was that tone that entered me as nothing in her voice had ever done before and impelled me to the airport.

A plane circling, first over blackness, then over gridded streets and runway lights. Circling down over long faintly illuminated parallelograms. It must have rained earlier, for as we came over the runway in the final descent, the tarmac was slick and dark. One could see reflections of our winking landing lights, of wing under wing, as though a black world to which we ultimately belonged were reaching up to claim us.

From the terminal, I found a taxi, which carried me again up into the air, over the concrete and asphalt ramps and the outbuildings and then down along the bay, over the causeway to the streets where I had grown up.

There, in the dark avenues of South Beach, palm fronds overreached the sidewalks and the fragrance of blossoms embedded in the fine humid air was funereal, night jasmine especially, as overpowering and thick as I remember it. I was coming home, back to where I had already died at least once.

It must have been two in the morning when the cab pulled up to the entrance of my parents' apartment house. The building was mostly occupied by aging retirees, and the halls gripped one with their poverty and death. A peculiar bitterness to the American dream that occasionally savaged the placid eyes of its residents as they stared out of faces masked in leathery sunburnt skin.

The door of my parents' apartment was off the latch, the handstained white enamel by the doorknob with its faint greasy stains curiously personal. The panel of the inner door was unhooked, slightly ajar, sending thin beams of light toward the dirty carpet of the hallway.

In the apartment, my mother had left the light on, and as I came into the front room, I could hear the TV in her bedroom playing, low and scratchy, as though someone were running a fingernail across a chalkboard. Her door too was ajar, and I could see, in the TV's spectral light, that she had knotted herself with the bedding into a small ball. She was sound asleep, snoring loudly as though possessed by dreams and terrifying night thoughts. There was something achingly pitiable about her lying there, her knees tucked up under her. She was doubled up like some poor creature brought from the ocean's depths which had curled about itself for comfort in its loneliness. Her black hair, which I could now see gleaming dully in the offlight, lashed about her features like weeds on the margins of waves. My father was nowhere to be seen.

JOURNAL ENTRY

Miami Beach
—the surgical waiting lounge of
Mt. Sinai Hospital
16 Jan 1979

Arrived yesterday, obtained a rental car and drove straight to the hospital. Sky slightly cloudy, the sun shining on the hotels as I crossed the bay, the flat white walls like the teeth of someone with a bright ever-fixed smile.

My mother looked good, rested. I stayed an hour, arranging some business matters, then went downtown to the Home to visit with my father. He was there, at the opening doors to the elevator, sitting in his wheelchair as though expecting me. He recognized me at once, yet, as with the last visit, he seems to have deteriorated further, unable to carry on a conversation or complete thoughts.

Went back to my mother. Her hospital roommate, an elderly Austrian-American woman who had suffered a stroke, asked me to write a letter for her since her right arm was paralyzed.

I talked with my mother for awhile. She shows nothing of fear or pain. Other patients on the floor cry and moan, but then, in my mother's presence as they look into her room or see her in the halls, they fall silent, ashamed of their complaining. I remember having read in some book on English painting that Queen Elizabeth I laid down a rule that no dark shadows should appear on her face in portraits.

The next morning, I talk to my father's doctor. My father has lost ten pounds since my last visit. He is down to 110, has taken to eating sparingly. One senses he has lost this world and now floats in one of his own making. Most of the day he sits in his chair, arms clutched like a praying mantis, half asleep. When his eyes open they are dark and glistening and he seems to be looking down a long tunnel. . . .

[Hastily scribbled note: Zev-JNF. Two pints of blood for Ma. If not, call R. S. from Democratic club.]

In the apartment, the tawdriness of my parents' collection of books. Old middlebrow novels, a Bible that looks as though it had never been opened, an Atlas, leather-covered, of the Cuban province of Camaguey, dedicated to Señor Peter F. Heller, *un hombre tranquilo gentil.* A copy of Stella Adler's *A House is Not a Home* suitably bound in a red cover—this was a book I read in secret, and the thought now reminds me of the purgatory of childhood. A large manila folder in which I found a poem of mine (1948–49), perhaps my first:

Precious Things

A precious thing
    in China is Tea
But Mother is
    Most Precious to Me

JOURNAL ENTRY

. . . she won't let anyone feel sympathy or sorrow for her—blunts those who want to "bless her" or weep at her misfortune. I gave her a big hug and told her I loved her—but no sooner had I had my arms around her than she was telling me "not to begin that stuff." "Alright Ma," I said, and I went out of the room as they were wheeling her off in the other direction. We had parted with great but moderated dignity as if nothing out of the ordinary was going to happen. Her attitude has put me quite at ease and I found I could actually sleep last night.

IN ELEGIACS, BIRDS OF FLORIDA

Gulls

Mother, those last vistas: you perched in the apartment which overlooked the wrinkled bay and the city whose patterned lights on the far shore resembled constellations. Near death, the whole world became a reading. So you too, father. At the home, I watched with you the palm fronds wave idly outside your room. Your eyes seemed to follow shadows on the walls, mind traceries, glints and powder darks, fan waverings of now and past, sea anemone, coral branch, yielding design but inarticulate.

Short stroll between you two, about the distance gulls will leave around a solitary walker who, at sunset, skirts the water's edge. A step too close either way and a gull will fly off, then another and another, to bob offshore on black water. Always a further horizon to inscribe a dividing line, a last blaze way out that catches the surf's turned edge. Before the salt nest of tombs, this consolation.

Flamingoes

Are nearly a secret. Half gawk, half grace, their thin legs hold them unsteadily erect. They teeter on non-being. A flock, they move as one outlandish pink-feathered thought. Something like the mind's repository of hosts and legends, their passage through the world, the double helix's cosmic joke: herd, family, tribe—how dead shades in groups are driven across the universe.

Snowy Egrets and Herons

Are ubiquitous. They fish in the inland canals behind the great hotels or at bayside, near backyards and docks of pale white homes. I have seen them hang silently in trees, eye's gift, sacs of tissue-papered fruit, the kind one buys for funerals. At sunset, they march their young across the highways and the TaMiami Trail, their nests in sleepy willows and cypress. With the beat of their wings, they have made the Everglades the other side of Lethe. They roost too beside the airport, calm and self-involved, standing at runway's end in shallow puddles amidst their own reflections.

Mind Birds

With my son, sitting in the park in Miami after a trip to the Parrot Jungle, we conjured up invented birds: the Guantanamo Guano Dropping Bat, the Elixir Eider whose feathers could stuff waterbeds, the Woid Boid, the Brooklyn poet's finest fowl.

I imagine, too, the Memory Bird—O synapse that can scribe its following arc! It circles over these peopled beaches of Hades and Limbo like the fabulous Garuda, a bird which never lands nor rests. Such a creature is too expensive to feed or tame or bring to earth to lay its unblemished egg of certainty. Still, at its highest flights, its claws tear at one's heart and liver more viciously than the eagles of Prometheus.

JOURNAL ENTRY

Tena called around nine o'clock with the sad news. Earlier in the evening, my mother, lying on the bed, began coughing and gasping for breath, becoming cyanotic. Her mouth was open and Tena could see fluid welling up in her throat. In wild desperation, she grabbed a plastic straw and tried to suck the fluids out of my mother's throat so that she could breathe. But it was to no avail. In a few moments my mother's life was at an end. My sister wept, I tried to comfort her, finally she calmed down and we talked about details: funeral home, I'd be there on the first plane in the morning, etc. I hung up and cried myself, thinking of my mother's rich but painful life, of my sister's courage and devotion, the image of her trying to save my mother, which would be with me for the rest of my days.

The cemetery and the crematorium lay out beyond the airport, and as we drove along the roads bordering the great runways, huge jumbo jets swooped down over us, shaking the ground and the car. As we pulled up to the crematorium, the bright sun caught the pale wisps of smoke rising from the tower of the chimney. Inside, we were met by a slim, bearded young man who was dressed in army khakis. He had been a Green Beret, he told us, speaking with a kind of strange cheer, while we were plunged in our grief, which he obviously did not notice or was inured to. He looked more than a little crazed in the eyes, smiling and insisting, before we went off with my mother's ashes, that we see what the crematorium amounted to. He walked us past the tracks that led to the furnace doors and to the bone-crushing machine. Here, what the fire had not reduced to ash was noisily ground into a fine powder. Holding a little dusting brush, he made hand gestures, indicating to us the precautions he took so that none of the fuliginious products of one corpse were mingled with another. There was to be no inordinate intimacy among the dead. At last, we drove off with our little box in which, in a small plastic bag, was contained all that was left of my mother's physical remains. The little pouch was about the size of a bean bag and indented easily when a finger was pushed against it. The color was pale, reddish, like sand, except it was infinitely finer and softer, almost like talc.

What my mother had asked, to have her ashes scattered over my father's grave, was, of course, illegal, there being a law against disposing of human remains by other than officialdom within the Miami city limits. Her plans for herself, or what was left of herself, were further complicated that particular day, for out there, at the cemetery and in the surroundings, the as yet sparsely populated areas of Miami, a good gusty wind was blowing. But we had come prepared for such contingencies. My sister and I had brought a plastic quart jug full of water and a bouquet of flowers.

We entered the cemetery grounds and drove slowly down the long lugubrious rows of plaques half-buried in the earth (there were no headstones allowed here, death had brought everyone to the same level) until we reached my father's grave site. His grave marker had not been placed yet, and there was only a small iron pipe holding a plastic bracket with his name on a piece of paper inside. We got out of the car and knelt by the gravesite, immobilized in our intentions by the close proximity of a man on a motorized tractor who was raking cut grass from the borders of the roadways. At last, after what seemed an endless time whipped by the wind in our meditations, the tractor moved off. Tena took the pouch of ashes and, opening it, nestled it among the flowers of the bouquet. As she moved up the length of the grave scattering the ashes over the grass-thin ground, I followed behind her, drizzling the water as best I could over the ash, over the calcified flesh and bone of my mother, some of which blew off even as it came from the pouch. Despite the wind, the sun suddenly seemed unusually hot. We stood over the grave laughing and crying while I recited a poem I had written for their fiftieth wedding anniversary.

Thus we had fulfilled the last wishes of my mother. Now a current of wind played over her ashes, the air shimmered over the baking ground making a mirage of trees off in the distance. Now we were orphans and our parents' lives, their time on this earth with its tangled meanings, was also becoming a mirage.

JOURNAL ENTRY

Miami, The Fountainbleau
22 April 1987

So much has happened. Our buddhist teacher, Trungpa, died on 4 April. Jane's mother, a few days later, nearly on her own birthday. State of mind at loose ends. One fears for lost teachings and teachers. I went to the Guru Yoga sadhana, tears in my eyes, but no particular desire to see Rinpoche in samadhi or to go to his cremation.

And now here, on Miami Beach again after so many years—today, I will visit my father's grave at Lakeside.

7:55 AM. I can see the beach, the ocean, the boardwalk from my window. A few joggers on the sand, a man fishing with a dropline. A mile or two off-shore, a line of tankers and cargo ships in the seaways, waiting to enter the Port of Miami. The odd postures and steps of people "walking" for exercise on the boardwalk. A woman doing calisthenics. Air of desertion, of single-ness. Lonesome and out of contact.

There is the climate. It has not changed. The heat comes with an ocean wetness; on the driest days, there are minute spindles of gold-flecked dew on the grasses and in the air. I helped a young woman from Provo, Utah. She was walking along Collins Ave. "Do you know this area," she asked?

I told her that I did. Her problem: tomorrow her friends would be arriving and what they most like to do is visit shopping malls and she hadn't found any yet. A pretty woman, but with a certain vacancy induced by being in a resort?

How to fill such a vacancy? This could be Miami Beach's theme. Consider the names of the hotels: Sans Souçi, Eden Roc, the Fountainbleau (where I am staying), Copacabana, Sea Isle, Lido, Greenbrier, Triton, Lucerne, Nautilus. Here, the power of the name, not to invoke but to create a false intimacy. The grandeur of the lobbies. I asked the hotel concierge where the nearest bookstore was. "Not on the Beach," he told me. "You'll have to go to Coral Gables."

Miami
23 April 1987

No going to convention sessions this morning. I'd reserved the day to visit the sacred sites of my childhood. Drove a rented car out to visit my father's grave at Lakeside. He is buried in the "Jerusalem" section, one of the many areas of the cemetery reserved for grave-markers that are flush to the ground. My father's plaque is bronze with a bevelled edge. There, chiseled out in the center, is a menorah with olive branches radiating out toward the corners. On the plaque is inscribed:

PETER F. HELLER

1904 – 1980

Beloved Husband of Martha

Beloved Father and Grandfather

What sign of my mother who did not want to be buried?

Lakeside is laid out opposite a large business and industrial park, a duty-free, tax-free zone for the booming city of Miami. Enormous semi-tractor trailers negotiate the narrow two-lane road along with visiting mourners. One leaves the dust of the road and crosses a little bridge over a drainage ditch to enter the cemetery. An odd, empty space for the most part; the cemetery seems to be, appropriately, an event about to happen.

Since my father's burial, rules have slackened. It seems now there are a number of ways to be interred in Lakeside: Under a flush marker, as with my

father, which recedes deeper into the close-cropped grass. Or under a regula-
tion-sized headstone in areas on the fringes of the cemetery. There, the stones
are packed close together and, in the haze, resemble herds of grazing brown
sheep. At the very center of the cemetery are enormous three-story vaults,
ossuaries with large overhangs for above-ground burial. Oversized storage
lockers, they look swiped from a railway station. The walls are rough concrete,
unfinished and harshly square, chaste and gloomy.

Here, death's democracy is morosely accomplished. In my youth, I hated the
idea of funerary pomp and mortuarial display. But Lakeside makes me think
again. The lack of distinctiveness, of variant, of some figure of excess, destroys
the memory of those who died. It affects the language of memory. The word
beloved *which had a certain potency is here merely a redundant trope,*
stamped on every other plaque. And the flatness, terminating in views of the
distant industrial park, reminds one of a military parade ground. The
mourner is diminished. The lone person that day on this vast expanse with
only a small shade tree for company and the sound of the truck noises far off.
No sign, no key by which to enter specific memories, nothing to jog a particu-
lar, to, in effect, mourn a person.

I stood over my father's grave and sought in the bronze details for
flaws. I read the words and the dates over and over in the hope that I
might discover in the bare, clichéd object the resonances by which to draw
him back to me. I looked at the surrounding grass and wondered whether
molecules from my mother's bone and ash had entered into the clipped
green shoots.

I drove back to the Beach. Worked my way from the past toward the
present. At 15th and Washington, I turned down the block and stopped
before The Hudson Arms where I had first lived. The dead man's skin tree
was still there and the patio where I had played with Alvin and Amy B.,
but the low wall that I skinned my knees on and the stairs leading to the
bookie parlor that everyone knew about were all gone. So were the silver
painted gas pipes that I used to play on. The coral colored paint of the build-
ing was peeling, but then it had always been peeling. Where had Yvonne
gone, the daughter of the landlord, and what had become of her older brother
who used to torment us? And who slapped me once for squirting him with
water from one of those fake flowers. I remember the newspaper we used to
put out, printed on a hectograph with its vile-colored shimmering jelly, the
Hudson Arms Gazette. The blue lines of the typing in the gel, the chemical
smell which clung to the paper which curled and yellowed in the following
days. The Hurricane parties . . .

I am trying to think back, realizing that though I have not been overtly concerned with origins, I have broken into time with each thought and let my personal story possess me for a moment. And yet, this order of speech and thought written out here, this dismembered and disjunctive meditation of a memoir, has at least one thing to commend it: it is not, it cannot be, the language of my past.

In this sense, its true audience is not a public, nor my peers, not even my own wavering consciousness which seeks always, in everything I write, an adventitious apothegm, a rubric, a cruel truth by which to live. No one living or to live constitutes my readers. The only true ones are my dead parents, for if they are responsible for everything conditioned about me and therefore capable of making a nullity and wasteland of so much that I resist, yet, in the most important sense, they are the origin of a life that has sought out in the above writing, the grounds of saying something they could not condition. I am their son, but only by trying to create that separateness and difference. So this work attempts to engage them in a conversation, which means to try to speak with them as equals, to write between these two self-imposed injunctions: *Remember that you were a slave in Egypt*—Deut. 32:7 and *The writing of history is a method for getting rid of the past*—Goethe

JOURNAL ENTRY

3 June 1993
New York City

He could not meditate on death, which he did not know. He could think about illness (or dying?), about that decay before one's eyes which is visible and which can be imagined through one's own fevers and flus, through one's injuries and hurts.

He understood his parents' deaths as at least a kind of closure while all the other lessons about "death" invoked only false nostalgia, sentimentality, and guilt. He understood that the only logical response to a closure was to evaluate what had come before. The "value" of a death, of a closure, can only be an utterance of sorts.

BORN IN WATER

Born in water. I was born in
my mother's water and washed out
into the world from the burst sac.

When my mother died, we respected her wishes,
collected her ashes at the crematorium,
then spread them on the grass over my father's grave.

And because the wind was blowing,
we poured water from a plastic pitcher,
and added water from our eyes
so the ashes wouldn't blow away
but seep into the ground.

Mother and father, as on the day
I was conceived, mingled together.

Works Consulted

In a sense, everything that I have read, heard, or been whispered to about, including all the poets whose work I have absorbed, has influenced me. So why—*pace* Jorge Luis Borges—leave out of a list of works consulted the tints of the sky each day or the sights, smells, and feelings of an afternoon or those of the other 22,693 afternoons that I have lived? In other words, as I have suggested earlier, what couldn't be placed on such a list as this? Here, in the interest of finitude and recognizing that this book is anything but scholarly, I am limiting the citations to those texts that are mentioned or have exerted such a direct and palpable effect on the writing of this memoir, that readers may want to explore further. There are omissions, and knowing full well that such omissions are bound to give offense, I beg forgiveness from the long list of authors living and dead whose writings I have failed to mention.

Asherson, Neal. "The Borderlands" in *Granta* No. 30, 1990.

Benjamin, Walter. *Illuminations*, Schocken, 1969.

———. *Reflections*, Schocken, 1978.

Biale, David. *Gershom Scholem: Kabbalah and Counter-History*, Harvard, 1979.

Bloom, Harold. *The Breaking of the Vessels*, The University of Chicago Press, 1982.

Celan, Paul. *Collected Prose*, Carcanet, 1986.

———. *Last Poems*, North Point Press, 1986.

Delbo, Charlotte. *Days and Memories*, The Marlboro Press, 1990.

Derrida, Jacques. *Of Grammatology*, The Johns Hopkins University Press, 1976.

Donoghue, Denis. *Warrenpoint*, Knopf, 1990.

Felstiner, John. *Paul Celan: Poet, Survivor, Jew*, Yale University Press, 1995.

Finkelstein, Norman. *The Ritual of New Creation*, State University of New York Press, 1992.

Finkielkraut, Alain. *The Imaginary Jew*, University of Nebraska Press, 1994.

Friedländer, Saul. *When Memory Comes*, 1979.

Gilman, Sander. *The Jew's Body*, Routledge, 1991.

Gorky, Maxim. *My Childhood*, Penguin, 1966.

Hamburger, Michael. *The Truth of Poetry*, Harcourt Brace Jovanovich, 1969.

Handelman, Susan A. *Fragments of Redemption*, Indiana University Press, 1991.

Hill, Geoffrey. *The Enemy's Country*, Stanford University Press, 1991.

Hoffman, Eva. *Shtetl*, Houghton Mifflin, 1997.

Joyce, James. *A Portrait of the Artist as a Young Man*, Viking, 1964.

Kristeva, Julia. *Desire in Language*, Columbia University Press, 1980.

Leiris, Michel. *Manhood*, Jonathan Cape, 1968.

Levi, Primo. *The Drowned and the Saved*, Summit Books, 1988.

Levinas, Emmanuel. *Difficult Freedom: Essays on Judaism*, The Johns Hopkins University Press, 1990.

———. *The Levinas Reader* (Edited by Seán Hand), Basil Blackwell, 1989.

Mandelstam, Osip. *The Prose of Osip Mandelstam*, Princeton University Press, 1965.

Merleau-Ponty, Maurice. *Sense and Non-sense*, Northwestern University Press, 1964.

Milosz, Czeslaw. *Native Realm*, University of California Press, 1981.

Morse, Jonathan. *Word by Word: The Language of Memory*, Cornell University Press, 1990.

Nabokov, Vladimir. *Speak Memory*, Putnam, 1966.

Ong, Walter J. *Orality and Literacy*, Metheun & Co., 1982.

Oppen, George. *Collected Poems*, New Directions, 1975.

———. *Primitive*, Black Sparrow Press, 1978.

Perec, George. *W, or The Memory of Childhood*, Godine, 1988.

Rakosi, Carl. *The Collected Poems of Carl Rakosi*, National Poetry Foundation, 1986.

Reznikoff, Charles. *By the Waters of Manhattan*, New Directions, 1962.

Revault D'Allonnes, Olivier. *Musical Variations on Jewish Thought*, George Braziller, 1984.

Rozenzweig, Franz. *The Star of Redemption*, University of Notre Dame Press, 1985.

Rudolf, Anthony. *The Arithmetic of Memory*, Bellew, 1999.

——. *At an Uncertain Hour: Primo Levi's War against Oblivion*, Menard, 1990.

Scholem, Gershom. *On Jews and Judaism in Crisis*, Schocken, 1976.

Sohn, David. *Bialystok: Photo Album of a Renowned City and Its Jews The World Over*, Bialystoker Album Committee, 1951.

Starobinski, Jean. *Jean-Jacques Rousseau*, University of Chicago Press, 1988.

Steiner, George. *After Babel*, Oxford University Press, 1992.

——. "Our Homeland, The Text" in *Salmagundi* No. 66.

Yerushalmi, Yosef Hayim. *Freud's Moses,* Yale University Press, 1991.

——. *Zahkor*, Schocken, 1989.

Zable, Arnold. *Jewels and Ashes*, Harcourt Brace, 1991.

Zukofsky, Louis. *"A,"* University of California Press, 1978.

——. *Complete Short Poems*, The Johns Hopkins University Press, 1991.

——. *Prepositions: The Collected Critical Essays of Louis Zukofsky,* University of California Press, 1981.

A Note about the Type

The text of this book is set in Adobe Caslon, which is based on Caslon Old Face, a classic font designed in 1725 by English engraver William Caslon I and later refined in his typefoundry. The display type, Poetica Chancery, is an original Adobe script designed in 1992 by Robert Slimbach and modeled after the elegant Italian Renaissance handwriting scripts known as "chancery hand," or *cancellarescha*.